THE NINTH WAVE

THE NINTH WAVE

Love and Food on the Isle of Mull

C A R L A   L A M O N T

First published in 2014 by Birlinn Ltd
West Newington House
10 Newington Road
Edinburgh
EH9 1QS

www.birlinn.co.uk

Design and layout by James Hutcheson and Tom Johnstone

ISBN: 978-1-78027-244-3

British Library Cataloguing in Publication Data
A catalogue record for this book is available from the British Library

Set in Bembo with headings in Gill Sans at Birlinn

Printed and bound by Livonia Print, Latvia

CONTENTS

INTRODUCTION

This book is about sharing the beauty and bounty of the Isle of Mull, the second largest island in the Inner Hebrides, through the eyes of Ninth Wave Restaurant, a chef and a fisherman. The restaurant takes its name from Celtic mythology, which tells us that 'the land of other-worldly delights' lies beyond the ninth wave.

When the sun shines on Mull its magic is there for all to see, but even in the winter gales with the wind howling through the telephone wires, the island exerts a primal pull on the traveller.

My husband and I invite you to explore the adventures of island life with us. We'll welcome you into our kitchen, take you out to forage on a traditional Highland croft, drag you into the garden to dig tatties and whisk you away on our boat to sort crabs on the pier on landing day.

Ninth Wave is situated just outside the village of Fionnphort, at the end of a 17-mile peninsula that comprises the portion of south Mull named the Ross. The Ross, meaning peninsula in Gaelic, is home to the villages of Pennyghael, Bunessan and Fionnphort and the outposts of Carsaig and Camas.

You will find Ninth Wave on a traditional Hebridean croft brimming with wild flowers, thyme and sorrel. We sum up our ethos as 'Hedonism on a Plate; where luxury meets sustainability'. As much as possible is made on our croft from the kitchen garden and foraged wild foods: from decadent handmade chocolates to fresh baked bread, chutneys and bramble marmalade to meadowsweet ice cream and black elderflower sorbet. During the last twenty years, most of our seven acres has been allowed to revert to its natural state. Since the land has been sheep-free, the indigenous plants and bees have not only come back, but natives like meadowsweet and purple loosestrife have flourished.

Signature dishes such Warm Smoked Crab Soufflé Cheesecake and Hand-dived Mull Scallops with Pernod, Garden Chard and Lobster Caviar await you as you follow the winding track to the restaurant.

Seafood is a big deal at Ninth Wave, and as such Jonny and his fishing boat have an integral part to play in what we do. Succulent lobster, crab, langoustine, hand-dived scallops and fish are often caught only hours before appearing on your dinner plate.

John, a Scottish fisherman, will not only catch your lobster and crab on his wee boat the Sonsie, but will also be your waiter and wine steward for the evening.

Ninth Wave restaurant is proud to be on one of the most extraordinary islands in the world. With over 300 miles of stunning coastline, Mull is known for its wilderness areas, wildlife and dramatic scenery. It is an island of contrasts: from the mystery of the Loch Buie standing stones to the sweeping sands of Calgary Bay, from the boulder-strewn cliffs at Gribun to the chocolate-box charm of Tobermory, from the pyramid peak of the Ben More to the wind-scoured heaths of Fionnphort.

Mull is a chef's delight if you know where to look. Its damp climate, moderate temperatures and plethora of habitats offer good growing conditions for lots of tasty flora, seaweeds and fungi. The island hosts a wonderful range of aromatic flowers, vibrant plants, juicy shoreline shoots, and super-fresh shellfish that make for some phenomenal meals. This is an island created to make a chef happy.

My first sighting of Mull, like many people's, was the brooding pile of Duart Castle seen from the Calmac ferry. As the boat came in, it was cold and the sea mist had gathered, making everything look very Scottish and romantic. My first real feel for Mull came as we sped along to Fionnphort on a bus, which was clearly driven by a madman with a death wish. The bus quickly threaded through misty pine trees on a twisting road that was just

wide enough for one vehicle. As we travelled down the single track road I noticed that quite a few cars with foreign plates completely ignored the passing places, forcing the bus to reverse several times.

As we entered the pass through the great hills, the terrain changed and the trees disappeared. There was something different about this landscape, something tangible, older, as if you could feel a million whisky-breath exhalations hanging faintly on the air. Dramatic boulders littered the landscape and long grasses with the distant look of green, crushed velvet draped the hillsides. It was April and the hills were weeping. Spring streams cut deep slashes through their slopes. As each small white cottage swung into view, I imagined I could hear the tatties bubbling over the fire. No need to imagine the blackface sheep and shaggy, bracken-coloured Highland cattle, as they punctuated the wilderness with joyful regularity.

In Canada I had never experienced this great age, this accumulation of purple-hued layers of the past laid one atop the other like a mysterious historical millefeuille. It felt to me like a sense of belonging, a homecoming. That feeling of connection to this island's past has never left me and it is the foundation upon which my love of Mull and its food has grown.

Even rattling along at quite a pace the bus journey takes almost an hour and I was getting hungry as usual. I'd stopped at a bakery in Oban where they assured me a scotch pie was just what I needed for a travel snack. How authentic. I pulled the round, rather severe-looking pie out of its brown paper bag and bit into it with enthusiasm. Oh dear. I was on a biscuit-tin of a bus pushing 60 miles an hour, in the middle of nowhere, with my entire mouth full of cold lard and pieces of leathery pastry. What was I eating? Surely this gelatinous devilry posing as a pie wasn't actually edible? I sat unhappily in my seat with my cheeks bulging. Perhaps if I waited, the unpalatable texture of this mystery filling would soften. But it was too revolting, I had to spit it out. So into the brown paper bag (which held the remains of the 'pie') it went. I would perform a proper burial ceremony if I ever got off the bus. That was my first taste of Scotland. It is a surprise that I didn't hightail it right back to Victoria, Canada. What kept me going was the thought, 'The food has to get better!'

We had passed through the pines, the glen and the eagle-watched waters at the Kinloch and were barrelling on towards Fionnphort and the ferry. Judging by the speed of the bus we were running late. There was an old stone bridge over a torrent up ahead. Since it was at a ninety-degree angle to the road the bus-driver slowed down a bit. My teeth were clenched and I was waiting for the horrible sound of the metal bus scraping along the stone sides of the bridge. Amazingly the screeching, tearing disaster I had imagined never happened. We were almost over the hump of the bridge. Just as the bus was turning back onto the road there was a strange thud and a noisy bleating over the sound of the engine. Nothing unusual could be seen out the huge front windshield. The driver looked in his side mirror and I looked out my window. Half-way along the side of the bus where the space between the bridge railing and the bus was at its narrowest, there it was. A huge sheep

with massive curling horns had tried to dash past the bus and got itself stuck. Norman the driver swore, turned the engine off and stood up. Straightening his shoulders, he deliberately brushed an unseen speck of lint off his pristine jumper, let out a sigh and stepped outside. The ewe was struggling to free itself and was in a panic. Norman, stoical now, approached the sheep from behind, grabbing its horns with both hands. Giving a great tug, he soon freed the sheep, turned it around and gave it a slap on the rump to get it headed in the right direction.

That was my first time journeying across the island, an experience I never fail to enjoy although I have done it over a hundred times. I had no idea then that I would make Mull my home. Thank God I'd kept on going to Fionnphort despite the bus ride, the suicidal sheep and the indigestible scotch pie.

LOVE AND LOBSTER IN A FIONNPHORT BOTHY

I was living in Victoria, Vancouver Island, in 1994 when my landlady told me about a job vacancy at a hotel on the Isle of Iona, Scotland. My colourful landlady (who made a good living at pretending to be Queen Elizabeth II) said that she'd heard of this job from a friend of a friend who had worked there. The hotel was looking for a meat-eating chef, as the entire kitchen staff was vegetarian. After sending my C.V. and labouring through an intensely weird phone interview about eating meat, I got the job. I was soon flying out to Glasgow for the beginning of the season.

I came over 7000 km to work on Mull's neighbouring isle of Iona. I was to work as an assistant cook at the seafront Argyll Hotel for six months. I loved the clear blue waters, white sands, atmospheric ruins and the friendly people. There was only one problem, no pool table.

In my Canadian city of Victoria, when not cooking I was a pool addict and the captain of a winning women's 8-ball team. I had played for hours each day and was suffering from withdrawal symptoms. I heard there was a pool table in the pub across the water at Fionnphort, so my first day off I ventured to Mull on the little ferry. I made my way up the tiny village street to the Keel Row pub and went inside.

It was a cosy wooden-floored, granite-walled room with a roaring fire at one end. I stepped up to the bar, ordered a cider and went to look for the pool table. I found it in a tiny back room beyond the ladies and gents. It was a miniature version of the real thing but I didn't mind. Better than nothing.

Unfortunately the whole point about playing pool for me is competition. There were no players in sight. I went back to the bar and asked the charming

PENNYGHAEL

owner, Andrew, 'Doesn't anybody play pool here? I came over from Iona to play.'

'Well,' he said, 'there's John or Peter. You'd catch them on Saturday, maybe.'

So I drank up, headed back to Iona and waited to get a Saturday off work.

A couple weeks later in June, I made it over on a Saturday. As before, the pool room was empty. I went and sat at an outside table to enjoy my cider in the sun. Soon after I heard a couple of guys at a table behind me, discussing books. They were arguing about who wrote *Dr Jekyll and Mr Hyde*. Minutes passed and they were still on about it, so I turned around and said, 'Actually, it's Robert Louis Stevenson'.

It was then I noticed the dirtiest fellow I'd ever seen. Dressed in what used to be a white T-shirt and faded jeans, this wiry, muscled man was covered in something like black axle grease. He even had smudges of it on his face. But shining amidst the mess like gems in a dung heap was a pair of the brightest blue eyes. Sparkling and full of humour, they pinned me to the chair. It was only for a second, and the sensation quickly passed.

That was my first sight of John (or Jonny as he became, as soon as he told me that no-one, but no-one, called him Jonny). He burred in his Scottish accent, 'You'll be the Canadian pool nut, then.' Not yet introduced to the island telegraph, I wondered how he'd heard of me.

'I must be,' said I.

'Are ye wanting a game of pool then?' asked John.

'With you? Like that?' I answered.

'That's right,' he said, waiting.

'O.K. then!' and it all began.

After I had thrashed Jonny at several games of pool over numerous pints he asked me over to his place the following week for a three-course dinner involving fresh lobster. Only later did he tell me that he had been advised (by no fewer than four people) to keep a look-out for a Canadian girl that wanted to play pool.

Jonny and I walked across the fields, by fallen stane dykes and over what was soon to become 'that dreaded plank' over the drainage ditch. He lived in the bothy, a squat byre-like farm building with gaping barn doors at either end and a barely habitable section in the middle. It was solid stone, with three-foot thick Caledonian granite walls and a rusted roof of tin that was full of holes. It had no hot running water, just a lone tap from a well; no central heating, just a sputtering open fire of peat.

During our first date the place kept filling in with peat smoke as down-draughts came through cracks in the chimney breast. We had to keep opening the door to let the smoke out and putting on our coats to offset the chill night air. We were sitting in a one-room rustic bachelor suite, kitchen and living room in one. The surroundings were less than salubrious, featuring an appalling brown fuzzy couch, a half-painted coffee table, cupboard doors of orange swirled glass and a tin bath hanging from a nail in the wall. I was dubious about the whole evening, having been asked on a dinner date by a grubby man I'd repeatedly beaten at pool in the village pub the week before.

My starter was served with a fisherman's swagger and a smile. It was octopus stuffed tomatoes. Three of them nestled on a brown earthenware plate. No fuss. I caught a whiff of oregano, thyme, butter-fried onions and the sea-salty freshness of octopus. John, with a tea towel slung over one shoulder, was waiting for me to try it. I took a small mouthful. The tangy delight of the vine-ripened tomato and the herby goodness were both divine. But what made this dish sing, wrapping it all in a big briny hug, was the creaminess of the octopus. From the taste I could have been lazing on a terrace in the Sicilian sun. I looked up into Jonny's face, which was still eagerly awaiting my verdict. I closed my eyes, smiled and took another mouthful. I was happy, he was happy.

The main course was lobster. I'd had Atlantic lobster tail from Nova Scotia, but never a *whole* lobster all to myself. What young girl could who worked as a cook could afford such decadence? This was the first time I was to witness what has now become one of our trademarks at Ninth Wave – Jonny's instructions on 'How to Get the Most out of Your Lobster'. He proceeded to tell me where to find the hidden tasty bits and overlooked treats.

'The tail you'll know . . . legs are a trauchle but worth it, the best part – but the whole thing's lovely, really.'

After thoroughly devouring the lobster, prodding every bit out with the end of a teaspoon and making sure I'd scooped out all the creamy bits, I licked my fingers, put my gloves back on and dreamily sipped at my wine (I was offered a whisky but it's something I just cannot drink). Despite the peat smoke, I could smell the rhubarb crumble in the oven.

The blissful mixture of garden rhubarb, Crabbie's Green Ginger Wine and crunchy oatmeal topping arrived at the table still bubbling. Ten minutes and a jug of pouring cream later we'd finished the lot. Together we'd braved the smoke, the winds, the 70s decor and I was in love. With the food or the fisherman, it was hard to tell.

JOHN'S TIPS
How to Get the Most out of Your Lobster

A GUIDE TO EATING A HALF LOBSTER

You will need a lobster pick and crackers
(or at a pinch a rectangular-ended teaspoon and a heavy spoon for cracking)

1. For the CLAW break the top mandible back against the hinge and use the spatulate (rounded) end of a lobster pick (or a small thin rectangular end of a teaspoon) to dig out the meat from inside. Then use the crackers to break the main part of the claw open to reveal the meat ready for picking out. For the rest of the claw arm, break at all the joints and pick out the meat in each section.

2. For the HEAD (carapace shell), break away from the leg unit by pulling all the legs together, while holding onto the shell. This shell has a thin layer of lovely lobster cream on the underside. Peel off the transparent membrane to get to it and don't mess about with cutlery, Get your thumb in there to scoop out this delectable essence of lobster.

3. For the LEGS, tear them off at the body and break at the joints. Squeeze each section with your fingers, from the thick end to the thin, to extract the threads of leg meat. The leg meat is the sweetest and tastiest meat on the beast.

4. For the TAIL, simply remove from the shell and feast on its heavenly splendour.

5. For the FAN end of the tail, remove the two side blades from the body by twisting sideways. The blade shell usually comes off empty, leaving the meat behind. If not, use the pick to extract it.

6. Above all, get stuck in. Don't be shy and enjoy!

The Humane Way of Killing Lobster

There are several ways to humanely kill a lobster. Putting the lobster in the freezer 20-40 minutes before cooking is one way. Another way is to plunge the tip of a sharp heavy knife-point straight down right behind the lobster's eyes in the mid-section of the head. I do not think there is enough lobster study evidence to say definitely that death by boiling, accomplished in several seconds, is preferable to freezing to death for a much longer period. Alternatively, put the chilled lobster in a large pan of cold, salted water and slowly bring it to the boil. It will be dead before the water reaches the boil.

OCTOPUS, PEA SHOOT AND GARDEN HERB SALAD WITH CHILLED TOMATO GASTRIQUE

This recipe evolved from Jonny's Octopus Stuffed Tomatoes, which were the first thing he ever cooked for me. This is an unctuous salad, enhanced by the contrast of the tart gastrique. Octopus meat is creamy with a pleasant mild flavour.

Serves 4-6

450g/1lb octopus, gutted and
   cleaned
60g/2½oz onion
1 tsp salt
2 sprigs fresh thyme
4 sprigs parsley
4 sprigs golden marjoram
2 curry leaves (or bay)

DRESSING
1 clove garlic, pureed
½ tsp ground coriander
1 tbsp marjoram, chopped
1 tsp mint, chopped
1 spring onion finely sliced
6 cherry tomatoes quartered
60ml/2fl oz Greek-style yoghurt
90ml/3fl oz crème fraiche
1 tsp lemon juice
dash chilli oil
sea salt and black pepper
chives and marjoram for garnish

GASTRIQUE
450g/1lb cherry tomatoes
25g/1oz butter
1 shallot, minced
15g/½oz sugar
2tbsp red wine vinegar

FOR THE OCTOPUS, place the first seven ingredients in a large pot. Cover generously with water and bring to the boil, then reduce heat to low, cover, and simmer for 1 hour or until tender. Remove octopus and allow to cool.

FOR THE DRESSING, mix all ingredients in a large bowl and season with salt and pepper to taste.

When the octopus is cool, remove the hard round beak in the centre of the tentacles if still present. Remove suckers and skin and discard. Slice octopus into roughly 15mm cubes and add to the dressing. Mix and marinade in fridge for 4-6 hours. Then add the peas and spring onions.

TO MAKE THE GASTRIQUE, heat the ingredients to boiling on a medium heat, then reduce to low and simmer for 15 minutes until tomatoes are soft. Use a hand-blender to puree the tomatoes. Press the gastrique mix through a sieve with the back of a spoon.

Serve a chilled spoonful of octopus salad in the middle of each plate and surround with a portion of the tomato gastrique. Garnish with fresh marjoram and chives.

MULL LOBSTER WITH GARDEN PEAS AND CROWDIE RAVIOLI

Sweet fresh peas with succulent lobster is a divine summer dish, perfect for garden parties. The use of traditional Scottish crowdie cheese in the pasta makes for a tangy alternative to ricotta.

Serves 4

PASTA DOUGH
220g/8oz semolina
180g/6oz 00 flour
5 eggs
6 sorrel leaves, pureed
a good pinch of salt

PASTA FILLING
I shallot, diced
560g/1lb 4oz crowdie
½ tsp butter
4 drops white truffle oil
I egg yolk
280g/9½oz shelled, cooked
   peas
sea salt and black pepper

2 lobsters, about 750g
450g peas
I tbsp butter
½ tsp lemon juice
I tbsp double cream
sea salt and pepper to taste
a handful of pea shoots

First, make the dough. Pile the semolina and flour on the worktop and form a well in the middle. Break the eggs into the well and mix with a fork, slowly drawing in the flour from the sides. When it is all incorporated, knead for about 10-15 minutes until the dough is smooth and silky.★ Cover the dough with plastic wrap and leave it to rest for 30 minutes. The dough can be rested overnight if necessary.

For the filling, fry the diced shallot in butter over low heat until translucent. Mash the crowdie with a fork until soft. Add to the rest of the ingredients with the shallots and mix well. Season to taste.

Dust a work surface moderately with 00 flour. Roll the dough quite thinly – 2-3mm, or use a pasta-rolling machine.† Cut the rolled dough into squares with a 5cm cookie cutter. Place a smooth, rounded teaspoon of filling in the middle of each. Using a pastry brush, moisten the edges with water and cover with another square of pasta. With your fingers, gently press the pasta together to seal, carefully removing any air pockets around the filling. The ravioli will not seal if there is any filling on the edges between the two pasta layers. Crimp edges of the pastry with fingers or fork to make sure they are sealed.

★When kneading, if you feel the dough is too dry, dampen hands with water and continue kneading.

†Cover extra dough not in use with a damp cloth to keep its moisture in.

Boil a large pot of salted water for the lobster.

Place a medium-sized pot of well-salted water on to boil for the peas.

Place the humanely killed lobsters in the large pot of boiling water and bring back to the boil. The lobsters will take 8 minutes to cook. After 4 minutes, add the fresh peas to the smaller pot of boiling water. Boil for 3-4 minutes until tender but still bright green. Remove the lobsters with tongs when the full 8 minutes have passed and place on a cutting board.

Place the ravioli gently in the lobster water and simmer for 3-4 minutes until the pasta is cooked to your taste.

Strain the peas and stir in the butter. Keep half of them warm, covered in the pot. Take the other half of the peas and whizz them up with the lemon using a hand blender. This should become a fine puree. Add the cream and blend again. Season to taste.

Remove the cooked ravioli from the water with a slotted spoon and place on an oiled plate. Cover with a pot lid to keep warm.

Place each lobster, belly-side up, on the cutting board. Holding the tail in place with one hand, take the point of a large, sharp knife and place it at right angles to the head so that the blade will slice down the length of the lobster. Plunge it into the centre of the lobster where the tail meets the body. Be careful to hold your fingers out of the knife's path. Press down firmly. Cut in half lengthwise. Rotate the lobster and repeat the procedure to cut the head in half. Separate the halves. Discard the gills and the dark intestinal thread that runs along the back of the tail. Remove the tail meat. Remove the empty tail shells from the head. Crack claws with a heavy spoon, the back of a heavy knife or pestle.

TO SERVE:

Place the head and claw half of the lobster on each plate.

Divide the peas among four plates.

Put ravioli on top of the peas.

Put a spoon of truffle dressing on the ravioli.

Place a half lobster tail on each ravioli.

Pipe or spoon the pea puree decoratively on the plate.

Garnish with pea shoots.

RHUBARB COMPOTE WITH PINK PEPPERCORN MERINGUES AND GALANGAL CREAM

A taste of summer. This combination of flavours really makes our garden rhubarb sing. All the components can be made ahead of time and assembled just before serving. Extra meringues and rhubarb compote will store well for up to a week, or can be frozen.

Serves 4

MERINGUES
2 egg whites
115g/4oz vanilla caster sugar
¾ teaspoon pink peppercorns, crushed
pinch sea salt

RHUBARB COMPOTE
600g/1lb 5oz rhubarb, cut into 2.5cm pieces
65-95g/2-4oz caster sugar
150ml black elderflower wine or rosé wine
¼ vanilla pod seeds
pinch of sea salt

GALANGAL CREAM
120ml/4fl oz double cream
½ tsp powdered galangal or ginger
1 tsp icing sugar, sieved
a drop of real vanilla essence

FOR THE MERINGUES:

Preheat oven to 150C/130Cfan/300F/Gas 2.

Put egg whites and salt in a grease-free metal bowl and whisk with a handheld electric beater until just stiff (not dry). To test, dip the beaters into the mixture and lift up – any white on them should stand up in stiff peaks rather than falling over.

Beating constantly, gradually add the sugar, until the mixture becomes very thick and glossy. Be sure to incorporate any stray sugar on the bowl sides.

Line a flat baking-tray with a non-stick baking sheet. Using a piping bag with a star tip (or a spoon) place 12 even mounds of meringue onto the prepared sheet about 3cms apart. Each meringue should be about 5cm wide and 2cm tall.

Place the meringue tray on the middle shelf of the oven, reducing the heat to 140°C. Bake for 35 minutes. Turn the oven off and leave the meringues to dry out in the warm oven for 3-4 hours. Store in an airtight container if not using right away.

FOR THE RHUBARB COMPOTE:

In a medium saucepan, combine the rhubarb, wine, vanilla seeds, salt and 65g/2oz of the sugar.

Bring to the boil over a medium-high heat, stirring occasionally. Reduce the heat to medium-low, cover

and simmer for 5 minutes, then taste the rhubarb for sweetness. Rhubarb and wines vary in sweetness, and ideally the rhubarb should still retain a hint of tartness in the compote.

Stir in more of the sugar if necessary and continue cooking, covered, for another 5 minutes or until the rhubarb is tender.

Straining the syrup into a small pot, put the compote into a sieve. Set the compote aside to cool.

Simmer the syrup on a medium heat and reduce until it has a runny-honey consistency, which should take 5-8 minutes. Set aside to cool.

In a mixing bowl, beat all the ingredients together on high speed until soft peaks form in the mixture. Chill, covered, in the fridge if not using right away.

TO ASSEMBLE:

Place two of the meringues on each serving plate. Pipe a 2cm high circle of galangal cream neatly on top of each meringue. Place a dessert spoonful of compote carefully on each cream circle. Top each with another meringue and dust with icing sugar. Decorate plate with syrup and serve.

THE CHOOKIE STANE OF AN IDEA AND THE RENOVATION

Our wee bothy was in such a bad state that I was desperate to move. After ten years of rustic facilities I was ready for some luxury, or even just hot running water and central heating. We had been half-looking for a place to buy and renovate into a house, but we just couldn't afford anything. We only had a few hundred pounds in the bank.

Then Jonny said, 'Why don't we stay where we are and turn this place into a restaurant?' And that was the birth of the idea that was to become our home, life and living. I knew even then that the land of milk and honey that lies behind the ninth wave in Celtic mythology would supply our name and ethos. Other-worldly delights indeed!

I was very naïve. Thankfully I was so naïve that I didn't realise that you couldn't get a bank loan for hundreds of thousands of pounds with no savings, no business experience, no contractor and few assets. I remember telling Jonny that now we had decided on the idea of renovating the bothy into a home and restaurant, we should be finished in six months. He said it would take at least a year. I rounded on him, saying that I was sick of his doom-and-gloom approach and his unnecessary pessimism. In fact it took seven years from his chookie stane of an idea until the opening day, 1 May 2009.

I knew what kind of restaurant I wanted. I was going to have all my best-loved things in one place, my idea of a perfect meal out. Teal bluish-green was my favoured colour, comfy seats were a must, lovely wooden tables, luxurious velvet, silver accents, unique, flavourful food and a cocktail menu to die for.

When going out to eat, the course I liked best was the appetizer or starter course. The choices for these are always so much more interesting than for

THE BOTHY — BEFORE CONVERSION.

the huge, starch-heavy main courses. If you want 3lbs of potatoes or a plate of pasta you can cook that at home. I wanted *taste*. At restaurants I often ordered two or three starters and left the main course out entirely. Also, in the few fancier French restaurants which I had eaten at in Canada, the menus seemed to be based around a variety of smaller-sized dishes that came at relaxed intervals. I preferred this continental way of eating to the old-fashioned rural British style of packing in as much as you can, as fast as you can, to get back to that pint in the pub.

We are still battling those ingrained habits and are up against the unwillingness of the average Brit to spend no more than a tenner on a meal. It is changing slowly here, but some people still choose price over quality, and the shops on Mull do a roaring trade in frozen and pre-prepared foods. But I decided to skip the massive main courses and adapt the continental approach for Ninth Wave's menu. I wanted the menu to be my dream menu. In the beginning, I built the menu around four, five or six starter-sized courses.

Planning menus was something I was used to. Garden design, interior decorating, furnishing and stocking an entire restaurant was completely new. During one idea-sketching session, I had the dining room kitted out with custom-made wrought iron couches bedecked with Sri Lankan silk cushions and artisan wrought-iron canopies overhead. I also had a raised dais with a pot-bellied wood-burning chiminea and bevelled glass doors separating the dining room from the tiny foyer. It soon became evident that are dining room was way too small for any of these over-the-top creations, and thank the universe for that! Our dining room still has an Asian feel to it, as I have been influenced by our world travels and the oriental population of west coast Canada, but it is modern yet comfortable.

The food too would connect to world culture, especially the orient. In Canada the Chinatowns in Vancouver and Victoria were my very favourite places to eat and shop for groceries. Forty percent of Vancouver's population is Asian and this has made a profound impression on me as a chef. Not concentrating on one food style in particular (modern British or Scottish for instance) is a dangerous way to approach a menu. It is easy for such menus to have no culinary focal point. The pitfall of offering a lot of disparate foods is that your menu, and hence your restaurant, will have no clear identity. I hoped that my individual cooking style and hedonistic personality would be the glue that held this idea together.

We went to the bank with our brilliant idea for Ninth Wave. We felt sure our own bank would fund us, as Jonny and I both had business accounts with them and had got loans from them before. Sadly, we were told that we needed business plans, architects drawings, planning permission, a building warrant and (what was to become our nemesis) the 'Bill of Quantities'. The bottom line was that we had little money, and restaurants are always considered a huge risk in the finance industry. A restaurant run by two novices out in the middle of a Hebridean moor with only change in their pockets was not only a risk, but insanity, judging by the look on the bank-manager's face.

Between the birth of the restaurant idea and the start of the build/renovation project, seven years passed. While red tape raged, Jonny kept stolidly fishing the shoreline of South Mull to help keep the funds in our coffers growing. He agonized over application forms with me and colourfully ranted against bureaucracy like a true anarchist.

I spent that time trying to save money for the project as well as doing the business plans, crazy paperwork, and the interior and exterior designs for the restaurant and house. I hired myself out as a relief chef on the island and worked on and off at Tiroran House Hotel, The Kinloch Hotel in Pennyghael (owned by our great friend Charles Pease Esquire) and the St Columba Hotel on Iona. I also catered for private functions under the

banner of Gourmet in Your Home, and worked a couple of seasons in a tiny eighteenth-century building on Iona that was then a antiquarian bookshop and is now a jam shop.

We were basically in limbo, treading water and saving the pennies until the gods of banking and building control saw fit to let us get on with it.

It cost all our savings and all our combined wages to pay for the architects, planning permission and the bill of quantities, a huge tome the size of a New York phone book, full of figures costing materials and labour for the build. Every nail and tin of paint had to be priced out. It would take a good month for a builder to complete just these estimates.

We would need to find a contractor who would be willing to take the job on. Contractors are hard to come by here. Good ones are even rarer and they often have to be booked years in advance. We thought we had a couple of them interested, but the bill of quantities and the fact that it came with all the difficulties of renovating a 200-year-old building, meant they backed out.

Through the grapevine we heard that Nigel, a builder from just down the road, had quit working on his mussel farm and maybe, just maybe, was taking on work. Nigel is a guy of contrasts: a Gaelic choir singer, fan of Buddhism, meditation and all things green, and an inveterate pinchpenny. He has a unique take on projects. Jonny knew him well, as he used to own the local boatyard at Bendoran that sadly no longer exists.

I spent months learning what net and gross meant, making spreadsheets, profit and loss sheets, cash-flow charts and writing a 50-page business plan complete with artist sketches, sample menus and wine lists. Before this I had never even balanced my own cheque book! I had to plan out and cost every fork, chair and piping bag in the restaurant. I made mood boards and consulted my old friend Richard, who used to be the manager of the Argyll Hotel when I worked there. He briefed me on everything from how much cutlery I would need to what type of napkins to buy. I was used to running a kitchen, yes. Being front-end manager and owner as well, no.

After six months of hard graft we were ready to go and get our loan from the bank man. The appointment was booked and off we went with a ton of papers, on the 10-hour round trip to Oban.

The loans manager was totally appalled that we'd spent £20,000 to get what he'd asked for. Pulling a face like a monkey's bum he said, 'That's all fine, but you'd need another £30,000 in your bank account before we'd even consider backing you'. It was a less than subtle way of telling us to piss off. It turned out that the Bank of Scotland's slogan 'A Friend for Life' was proving less than accurate. So we trawled around Oban pitching our idea to every bank in town, but there were no takers.

Days later we were moaning to our neighbour Derek about our problem and he suggested we try his bank. Triodos is a bank specialising in sustainable and environmentally friendly investments and is based in Holland. We had nothing to lose. We could do green. We changed our perspective slightly and focused on using recycled materials and eco-attentive heating and design choices. I rewrote the business plan and away we went to Triodos to ask for a loan. Amazingly, only six years after the birth of Ninth Wave as a concept, we had found a bank that would fund our build. Even so, we could never have managed the build without a huge grant from Highlands and Islands Enterprise, who as a rule don't normally back restaurant projects. Dear Nigel agreed to start renovating the old farmstead in August. Things were starting to go our way.

The Build

It was exciting. This two-room shanty would soon be turned into a restaurant. It would house the dining room, toilet, coat-closet, and storeroom. Our wee living space at the other end of the bothy would comprise a lounge, porch, bathroom and one bedroom with a shared kitchen between the two.

During the early work on our renovation we found out that there had been a Bronze Age settlement on our croft. During the time of the Scottish kings, the path taken by funeral processions and wayfarers going to Iona is believed

BEFORE AND AFTER THE BUILD

to have passed right through our narrow strip of land. How interesting and expensive this knowledge turned out to be. We were served with a watching brief, which required us to employ an archaeologist to supervise the bit of excavating we had to do for the development. As the bothy was built on a hill, we had to level the ground in front of the restaurant before we began the build. The cost of employing an archaeologist came as quite a shock at £1,000 a day. It should only take a day, unless of course we unearthed a hoard of gold, the Bronze Age settlement or St Columba himself. As we were only going to dig down far enough to the level of the 1800s none of these were probable. As it was, all they found was a load of buried fishing rope, some rotting corrugated iron and a crappy silver-plated Victorian spoon.

My friend Janet jokingly calls me the 'Goddess of Patience and Tolerance', but, boy, was I to learn some patience, and soon. During the winter build we had our share of hiccups: a water source appeared in the building while a trench was being dug for the underpinning, lovely granite walls had to be knocked down due to instability, materials vanished, we lost our rock fireplace to make space in the living room, the liquor-licensing people were schizophrenic, and Nigel had forgotten to hire a tiler. The foul weather that time of the year didn't help either.

We were disrupted by the build, stuffed into a small caravan or mobile home as I call it. It had a dodgy shower that alternated hot and cold water randomly, a sink drain that smelled like an over-cooked cabbage and an oven on which only one burner worked. We shared with mice, shrews and blackbirds that played relay races on the aluminium roof at 5am every morning. I didn't care. The end was in sight. I was to get my new place complete with all the mod cons. And we'd be in by May. There was nothing forty dozen chocolate chip cookies and a grain silo full of tea couldn't fix.

One day, at the beginning of the demolition stage, we looked out of the caravan window to see Nigel and his crew sitting under a makeshift shelter in the lee of one of the remaining stone walls. All three of them were hunched dejectedly under a flapping tarp in a gale with rain pouring down. They were trying to eat sodden sandwiches while their tea was blown out of their flask cups before they had time drink it. Jonny went out to them. 'Don't be daft. Come away in and get warmed by the fire.' They came inside the caravan, I made a fresh pot of tea and they enjoyed their lunch in relative comfort.

First to be demolished was the roof and old beams, leaving only a naked shell. One day, without much warning, all the unstable walls had been unceremoniously torn down and there was only a sad half of bothy left. The next morning found Nigel standing atop the interior stone fireplace wall, holding a wrecking hammer. This was another sad loss that we are still regretting. I know we'd give back the space if we could have our pink granite wall and fireplace returned.

The wildlife on the croft wasn't put out by the build in the least, however.

In fact, besides all the snipes, hen harriers, kestrels, owls, bats, hedgehogs and toads that were usually around, there were a few new visitors.

8 am on a calm cloudy day and Jonny and I were enjoying our morning coffee while looking out at the morning from the fish bowl window in the caravan. East-facing, this huge window framed the dawn breaking over our lower fields. I was about to down the dregs of my cup and head over the track, when something fast caught my eye. I saw something moving on the building planks that were piled haphazardly just below the caravan window. Jonny had noticed it as well and we took a closer look. Running up and down on one of the planks was a brown spotted bird with a grumpy expression and an open beak. Then out it came 'Creck-creck. Creck-crek.' The elusive and highly sought after corncrake had taken up residence under the caravan.

Many twitchers would pay for a look at a corncrake. Iona has a known population of these birds (Latin name Crex crex) but they are much rarer on Mull. This addition to the croft wildlife was noteworthy but annoying. Our bird made the cuckoo seem like a quiet soul. Jonny was standing leaning on the fence in front of the caravan one afternoon when the corncrake suddenly wandered out of a stand of waist-high apple mint. As Jonny stood still, the corncrake walked around his feet, pecking on the ground for food, and after several minutes then disappeared back the way it came. Our corncrake lived there for that summer and still comes back each year in April.

Many a day I came home from work to find a new scene before me. The first day of the build was spent prepping the building. I came home from the shop on Iona to see the remains of my beloved champagne-coloured velvet couch (that had been shipped all the way from Canada) smouldering on a massive bonfire. I cried that day.

To keep labour costs down I decided to help with the easier tasks. I was given the job of insulating the roof with Kingspan energy-efficient panels. A true friend, neighbour Derek, came over to help me. Derek had more experience than I in such matters and was in charge. Measure twice, cut once he advised. Wearing masks, we started in on the sawing of the the insulating board. My hair and face were soon covered with static-charged crumbs of Styrofoam. I finished up looking like a cross between a wine-sodden Santa and a rabid beagle. An outstanding academic and scholar, Derek could recite both modern poetry and quote Shakespearean verse to keep us entertained. Unfortunately that same brain could not keep track of a pencil, and we went through half a dozen in less than 20 minutes. We ended up tying a string from Derek's pencil to his belt-loop and he only managed to lose that once.

Because of some missing tradesmen I had to fast–track and learn how to tile and grout, calk and seal, nail and fill. When going over the dreaded bill of quantities before the start of the project, we agree to keep the price down by doing the decorating ourselves. Now in Canada, decorating means painting room walls, hanging artwork and putting up window coverings. Not so in Scotland. Apparently I had signed up to sand, stain, prime and paint all the baseboards, gable decorations, fascia boards, trim, doors and the entire exterior on the wood-clad extension. I was soon to be heard yelling over our shared fence, 'Derek can you spare a minute? Bring all the paint brushes you can find!'

The first few weeks of the build uncovered a number of unforeseen snags. I was on my way over from the caravan one weekend with a tray of tea for the guys when I heard shouts of alarm. I came into the shell of the framed building to find Nigel leaning on a shovel staring at a hole full of gushing water in what was to become our bedroom. He'd been trying to level out the dirt for pouring concrete and had unearthed a burbling spring. When I said I'd always dreamed of having a jacuzzi in the bedroom that wasn't quite what I had in mind. Not for the first time Nigel wished this ancient granite elephant of a croft would disappear so he could erect a 'Build by Numbers' new house. After more tea and biscuits a complex drainage outlet was rigged up and the concrete floor pad went in as planned. It is still slightly unnerving to think that there is running water underneath your floor, but hey, this is wet west Scotland. We're quite lucky really, as Derek next door has an entire stream coursing under kitchen and back porch.

THE BUILDING INSPECTOR

Sometime during the build I asked Nigel how many handrails we needed for the handicapped toilet facilities. Scratching his loveable tufts of hair he said he was sure that none were required. I said OK, but promptly ordered an industrial handrail on the internet.

To open, we needed to pass a building certificate inspection. We'd heard how difficult the junior inspector was and were dreading the inspection. He arrived late. He was a slight, stooped, bookish fellow with a pinched face. Thus started the saga of the handrails. He said we needed one in the bedroom but not in the toilet. We fitted the one I had bought 'just in case', onto the bedroom wall to the approval of the wee mannie. Ten days later he came back for a second inspection with his much nicer boss, who informed us that we didn't need the handrail in the bedroom but needed one in the toilet. While they watched, we removed the rail from the bedroom and put it in the toilet. Also, with only one day to go until opening, we apparently needed a drop-down rail for the handicapped in the toilet as well. Disaster. The head guy was very helpful and said that we could send him a photo of the installed special support rail when we got it, and he would be happy to sign off the build and give us our certificate. Unfortunately living on an island does have its drawbacks: one of them is the lack of specialist shops and another is long shipping times. We needed that certificate now. We needed that handrail now. We watched as the inspectors drove away down our gravel track.

I was desperate and had to think quickly. I could only dredge up one person we knew in the village who had one of these fold-down support rails in his house. A phone call later and Jonny was on the way to good old Bruce's council house in the truck. He ripped the rail off his toilet wall and sped back to the restaurant. Ten minutes later we had it installed and took a photo of it in situ. The photo was emailed to the warrant office; we took the rail off our wall, reinstalled it in Bruce's bathroom and had a cup of tea with him, and all before the inspectors had even reached the ferry to the mainland. We got our completion certificate the next morning and we could open on time. When our real handrail arrived a week later it was duly fitted.

Jonny did his bit to save money and had the backbreaking job of digging a trench around the rear of the building in November so we could pour a section of concrete to help secure what was left of our beloved stone walls. Our bothy was built right into the hillside for protection against the elements. The trench was between the boundary, which was a 7-foot high wall of earth

backing onto the beginning of Mary MacKay's croft next door, and our granite wall. The problem was that since the space was only 2 foot wide a digger couldn't be used. It's barely wide enough for one person, and I still have to lope along sideways like an orang-utan when venturing out the back to retrieve something I have mistakenly dropped out of the kitchen window. Jonny toiled in this space for days with a pick-axe, a bucket and a spade. It nearly did break his back and he was often seen scuttling crablike after a day's digging, muttering about underpaid slaves and massages.

On the first day of the trench excavation Jonny got a shock. As he put the shovel into an unbroken piece of grassy ground the top came off very easily. Uncovered was a huge ball of hibernating slow-worms. Slow-worms are rarely seen as they seek deep cover and hunt after dusk. I've only seen one beautiful bronzy specimen of this legless lizard in my twenty years here. The slow-worms were hibernating in this large ball in an underground burrow to keep warm. They were relocated to our upper field and no doubt help to eat the gardener's enemies.

The renovation was a long hard slog, but as happy parents are heard to say, 'It was all worth it, didn't she turn out well?'

Gleaning Experience

While the build was on, my life was in limbo. I'd quit full time employment and was trying to drum up extra cash with my home-based catering business 'Gourmet in Your Home'. The idea was that I would go into homes, mansions, castles and so on to cater for dinner parties, weddings and other events. It was stressful and just a bit wacko to try and run this out of our wee caravan, but needs must.

Once we catered a dinner and a picnic party at a large holiday house overlooking Glen Forsa. I had made spinach and feta tartlets, filled ciabatta rolls, prawn and papaya salad and strawberry shortcake for their family fishing outing, and a four-course gourmet dinner for eight. The house was very posh. After the Mull Scallops on Gingered Rice Noodles the diners

exclaimed that my cooking was as good as Le Manoir aux Quat'Saisons. I nodded and smiled and had no idea what they meant (until I googled it the next day). As I cooked in the huge kitchen that opened out into the glass-walled lounge, the owners chatted with me, asking questions about where I had worked before. I told them about working at the Argyll Hotel on Iona, at Tiroran House and more recently the Kinloch Hotel at Pennyghael. I casually mentioned that I'd just finished catering at the Kinloch for the Archduke Algernon --------, a relative of the Queen's. I mentioned that we called him the Chicken Man, because he was obsessed with all things chicken and requested it at every meal. I told them how charmingly eccentric he was about his chicken and the adventures we'd had with him. The lady replied,

'Oh, good old cousin Algy. He never changes! Tell him cousin Rosie was asking after him.'

While living in the caravan Jonny and I also catered a seafood buffet dinner and breakfast for Calgary Castle, way at the north end of the island. We had to prepare some of the food beforehand for the huge smorgasbord. That was quite an exercise in spatial planning, as I was cooking with only two burners and an oven the size of a shoebox. Calgary Castle is an impressive historic mansion with decorative crenellated towers set in 48 acres of woodland right beside a great expanse of white sand. We hadn't been keen on the four-hour return journey back to Fionnphort, but luckily we were offered a lovely room for the night, at the top of the great sweeping staircase of the Castle. Jonny was the waiter, bartender and my assistant in the kitchen. He had a pretty steep learning curve, making Duck and Cognac Pâté and Prawn and Dill Spring Rolls, serving champagne, re-filling trays in the great lounge and pouring drams. We fell into our four-poster bed well past 2am and had to get up at 6am to start preparing fresh croissants for breakfast.

It was challenging catering these functions, as I was always in a strange kitchen and didn't know what I was working with until it was too late to do anything about it. Once Jonny and I found ourselves in a tiny cottage up at Treshnish, catering for a large group of Italians. When we got there the electric cooker didn't work and all we had was an oil-fired Raeburn stove with an evil temperament. Somehow we managed to serve a load of Hebridean chowder, lobster ravioli, crab cheesecake and hot chocolate fondant puddings without a hitch. Everything took a bit longer than usual, but the Italians were ecstatic about all the fresh Mull seafood and said it was the best meal they'd ever eaten in Britain.

On the way to my restaurant dream I used to cook at the Fishermen's Gala Day which was held once a year, right on the ferry pier in Fionnphort. Me and my friend Mrs Slade hosted open-air cooking demonstrations during this summer celebration. We dressed in fishing-net tutus and fluorescent hats made out of orange floats one year and as galleon-esque mermaids with blonde wigs the next. We were adventurous and introduced the locals to such delights as Prawn and Pico de Gallo Tortillas, Mediterranean Octopus Salad and Five Herb Hebridean Chowder. As we dished up copious amounts of nosh and gave out cooking tips in the summer sun we drank several bottles of vino besides. Because of public demand we began a fresh food stand alongside the live cooking show.

We became known as 'The Two Not-so-Fat Ladies' at the yearly Bunessan Show, eight miles down the road. We sold out each year, whether it was Mexican, Moroccan or modern Scottish seafood we offered. I have vivid recollections of Mrs S. and me singing 'Speedy Gonzales' while brandishing a rather large banana pepper at Mr Neil MacGillivray, one of the oldest men on the Ross of Mull. We also were asked to have a picture taken with a very nice man who had just moved to the area one year. Both dressed as Carmen Miranda, we posed on either side of him, each giving him a kiss on the cheek. Little did we know that he was the new minister at Bunessan.

Another thing I learned from these experiences is that I love interacting with audiences and revel in the wild, circus aspect of it all. Since then I've tried video auditioning for the likes of Gordon Ramsay and Nigella Lawson, sadly all to no avail.

The local Scottish Women's Rural Institute asked me to give a lecture and cooking demonstration at the Fionnphort village hall. I had just got back from a culinary tour of South Thailand, and thought it would be a great opportunity to share the experience. When I pulled up to Creich Hall, my car was full of treasures brought back from the Land of Smiles. There was a two-foot high bronze Buddha, a bolt of gold-threaded cloth and boxes of exotic ingredients.

I set up the gas cylinder and cooker top on the trestle table and set to work displaying the plethora of green papaya, galangal, lemongrass, palm sugar, nam pla (fish sauce), fresh coriander and more. I put all the Thai oddities in tiny ramekins in a row at the front of the table so the ladies could come up to look at and taste them. Most of the women from the Institute had never seen any of these Asian ingredients before. With an audience of two dozen women from the Ross seated patiently on chairs with hands folded in laps, it was time to begin. I put some Thai flute music on the speaker and started making green curry paste for the chicken curry, frying green onions, green chillies, green peppers, coriander leaf, Thai basil, galangal and Thai shallots. The divine smell filled the hall. As I pounded, chopped and stirred, I recounted some of our travels to Koh Jum island and the holy city of Nakhon Si Thammarat. While waiting for the prawn head stock for the Tom Yung Kung Soup to reduce, I invited the ladies up to explore the ingredients.

At the end I served up the two dishes and handed out samples to all the ladies. Some of these ladies are very traditional and still consider rice and spaghetti to be 'foreign muck', so I had no idea how these pungent chilli-laden foods would go down. Then, Nan, a lovely and slight Bunessan woman in her 70s asked for more of the fiery Tom Kung Soup. That started a run on seconds. The usual exaggerated Scottish compliment 'Very nice indeed,' was heard and the whole night deemed a success. I handed out copies of the recipes and still wonder if they ever see the light of day.

After an eight-month build the scheduled opening day was looming. Nothing was going to set back that date. If I had to go and Indian mud wrestle with the officials at the Argyll and Bute Licensing Authorities I would.

The restaurant was due to open on 1 May 2009 and we were cutting it pretty fine with the main warrants and licenses. The budget was tight and the funding had dried up.

The last stage of the build to be done was the decoration. We couldn't afford an interior designer so it was another thing I'd have to do myself. It was the first time in my life I had free rein to go and style an entire set of rooms. I loved playing designer, and have to admit to being a bit of a control freak anyway. The colour theme was easy, my favourite colour, teal. This would also go with the sea-themed name and was different to most of the other new restaurants emerging at the time which seemed to be going for minimalist browns and neutrals, with a bit of lime green or caustic orange thrown in. Minimalist it wasn't. If Madame Over-the-Top was in charge, the décor was sure to be different.

I was awash with paint cards, tile samples, mood boards, flooring off-cuts and catalogues. Shopping on the internet to outfit a whole restaurant was challenging indeed. We didn't have a lot of money, but we spent it where the diner could enjoy it. The floors were a lovely eco-friendly bamboo which echoed the 'Arabian Sands' accent of the walls. The tables were top-quality chunky solid oak and the travertine marble sink and tiles in the toilet finished off the look.

The chairs were probably the single most important design element in the dining room. John and I hate dining on uncomfortable chairs. Our customers would be at their table for a good three to four hours and needed comfy seats. When buying chairs the only way to do it properly is to try them out. I found a great furniture company in Shropshire that had made several chairs I loved the look of. I phoned a friend in Warwickshire (Shropshire looked very close on the map) and asked if I could stay with her while chair hunting. She agreed to drive me to the chair warehouse the day after I arrived.

It took us a couple hours in her VW convertible but we put on some Edith Piaf and drove off into the sunshine. After we arrived in Telford I spent a good many hours sitting on chairs, looking at choices and playing touchy-feely with those huge books of luxurious upholstery fabrics. The trend was for insanely tall, rectangular chairs with leather upholstery. I always make a point of veering away from the norm. After playing musical chairs I finally decided on the most comfortable chair I could find, a simple backed chair with a classic roll top, and chose a teal waved velvet to cover them. Job done. I supposed my dinner guests would never know to what lengths I went to ensure their comfort.

Now I just had to find the perfect menu covers, foyer furniture, mirrors

and light fixtures. I wanted the restaurant's décor to reflect the international melange that is my cultural heritage as a Canadian. I chose hanging lamps from Tangiers and marble floor tiles from Italy. Every vacation we went on during the seven years' gestation period of the restaurant was spent gathering special items for it. We bought elephant loop cutlery, an amulet house and a good luck guardian in Thailand, fossil-embedded stone placemats from the Sahara desert and abundant masks and pottery from Sri Lanka.

I tried to keep control of my decorating impulses and not overfill the restaurant. I feel that our diners need some space to breath and a somewhat uncluttered atmosphere to enjoy the dining experience to its fullest. However, my love of all things steampunk has crept into the foyer in the form of a clock, barometer and weather instrument wall. I am still trying to find a place for a massive antique brass ship's compass, but probably never will.

47

OPEN FOR BUSINESS

Opening Night

The opening night of a restaurant is a very important occasion. It sets the tone and the feel for the whole restaurant, and as we all know, there is only one first impression. Thirteen years ago Ninth Wave was a mere breath of an idea, born out of hunger, longing and perhaps one too many ciders. 1 May 2009 was the beginning of our trading life, and what a night it was.

Our opening night was completely booked with our friends. At 18 covers it was maxed out. Never before had the village of Fionnphort, or indeed the Ross, seen such fine dining. Everyone was dressed to the nines and all in festive mood. Much champagne and numerous cocktails made the rounds. This was the real deal. Around here you only get one chance to impress. If you disappoint a local, all 500 island relatives get to hear about it in short order.

Kirsty, the youngest of John's daughters, had come over from Glasgow to help me in the kitchen. I was a bit shell-shocked after all the stress of latest developments; a delayed liquor licence, a protracted building inspection and a builder who'd gone off the rails, whispering 'I don't have any idea what to do next!' while staring off into space. The opening of Ninth Wave seemed to have coincided with some hormonal change in my brain. I was mentally unstable, euphoric one minute, weepy the next, one minute doing Speedy Gonzalez impersonations, and then muttering obscenities at Jonny the next. Kirsty was our rock and manned the pass, shouting out the orders as they came in. I did the cooking. The sea-urchin flavoured French onion soup topped with Mull cheddar and puff pastry went down a storm, as did the teriyaki Mull Highland beef fillet with julienne of garden veg. I wish I'd kept a menu from the opening night, but that was the last thing on my mind.

After the choccies and coffee had been served, I heard someone tapping a wineglass with a fork in the dining room, asking for silence. Jonny said my presence was required. I donned a less splattered apron, cleaned the melting mascara off my face and ventured into the dining room. John Noddings, who ran the only 4-star B&B in the village, was on his feet, wine glass in hand. He extolled my virtues, much to my embarrassment, and went on to give a wonderfully heartfelt speech about our new community restaurant, which ended in a teary-eyed toast. I felt much like crying myself. To think, our food and the place we had created could actually bring people to tears!

A Not So Average Day

During the season my work day starts between 6 and 7 am, depending on how much my assistant Fédra and I have to prepare. I pull on my chef's whites which have been lovingly pressed by our Fiona and toddle into the kitchen to begin writing the menu for the day. I base it on the veg that will be ready for picking and the various meats and seafood that will arrive throughout the day.

The menu rarely stays the same two days in a row. It would drive me mad with boredom if I cooked the same thing all the time; besides, the whole ethos of our restaurant is to plan the menu around the fresh ingredients as they are available. I may know that after a trip to the veg garden yesterday that there is a bunch of courgette flowers that will be ready for picking, and put Seafood Stuffed Courgette Blossoms with Herby Hollandaise and Garden Petal Salad on as a second course.

Next I write the prep list on the white board next to the stove, so we can easily refer to it as we whirl around. I start fermenting the yeast for Flooby (our daily bread) before beginning to prep. Flooby is reincarnated every day in his seaweed Zen form. Jonny gets the day-old bread in his lunch sandwiches to take out on the boat. The prep list can often have 30 to 40 things on it, plus garnishes. It's a punishing amount of work, and some days

I don't get to stop for breaks or meals but continue working on until service and dishes are finished at 11 pm. My record is a seventeen-and-a-half hour day with no breaks. Chefs the world over all work long, stress-filled shifts, it's just part of the job. I laugh out loud when watching TV shows about people who give up their 9 to 5 day jobs to buy restaurants or become chefs for the good of their family or to spend more time with the kids. Good luck with that.

I never make a cuppa right away but get stuck right in, often forgetting even to put on an apron. Around 8 or so Jonny rolls into the kitchen to make his breakfast fry-up and lunch. It's then that he makes me my first cuppa of the day. I'm usually up to my eyeballs in making seafood stock, baking meringues, proving Flooby and marinating venison. My hands are always busy and I habitually forget my tea after a couple mouthfuls, which drives Jonny crazy.

I then go out into the garden and pick the things like Mizuna greens and land cress that need several soaks and washes to get all the lovely black dirt from the garden off them. Jonny picks the remainder of the needed produce after he has eaten his breakfast. He loves going out into the garden and harvesting the rewards of his labours. The kitchen soon fills up with baskets of freshly dug tatties, fronds of spinach and kale, and/or peas/beans/beets, depending on the month. Eyes on hands and bubbling pots, I often trip over baskets of veg that have been strategically placed for my inconvenience.

If we have vegetarians in on the night, we aren't satisfied with offering them only one vegetarian starter and one main course only. The set menu is the same price as the regular menu, so I feel they should have the same amount of choice per course and the same amount of imagination and detail in their menu. We often get letters and comments from our kind vegetarian customers stating 'That's the best vegetarian meal I've ever had.' Our custom veggie menus give me the chance to showcase a lot of our garden produce along with specialty cheeses, and exotic ingredients brought back from our travels. Vegetarian menus have included:

Warm New Potato, Broad Bean and Mouli Salad with Strathdon Blue

Garden Chard and Fennel Cheesecake with Red Onion and Fennel Jam

Buckwheat Blinis with Beetroot and Fresh Horseradish and Goats Cheese Crème Fraiche, Japanese Pickled Plum and Mibuna Salad with Sesame and Nori Tuilles

We also do menus for vegans and gluten-free (when given a day's notice) as there are an increasing number of customers with these dietary requirements. I bake special bread and oatcakes for these guests fresh on the day.

Fédra comes in with her usual 'Good morning, how are you?' It's just a formality so she can gauge what mood I'm in and how the day is going from the atmosphere and level of chaos in the kitchen. Most days it is busy but sunny with only a chance of showers. Fédra then cleans all my mess away, does the

GATHERING MEADOWSWEET FOR THE KITCHEN

dishes, puts last night's napkins on to wash and gets going on the prep list. She is very patient so I give her long and involved items to make, like chocolate tart, layered jellies or fiddly chocolate decorations.

FIONA

Fiona, our cleaning lady (or aesthetic and antiseptic engineer as we call her), appears shortly after to do her thing in the restaurant. No pinny for this well-read fashionista. Fiona often looks as if she is on her way to a gallery opening (sporting charm bracelets and nattily-tailored jackets) instead of a morning of cutlery polishing and table setting here. She is a whirling dervish of cleanliness, a stalwart supporter, a good friend and does us proud.

As soon as my hands are covered in bread dough or something else really messy, the phone calls from wine and food suppliers start to come in. Racks of Treshnish lamb have just come back from the island slaughterhouse, or Sandra has extra duck eggs today. Inverlussa mussels will be arriving on the service bus down by the ferry pier in an hour, and how many kilos of organic malthouse flour would I like for next week? And occasionally we get calls in the morning to look out for pigs/sheep/cows that have escaped during the night and are on the randan.

Sometimes we get to stop for a tea break at 11 am. That's when we like to sit outside in the small caravan garden and enjoy the view. Often passing villagers who are out for a walk get invited to stop, or Michael Williams (courier/delivery man extraordinaire) might stay for a chat if he isn't running for a ferry.

FÉDRA

Whittling down the list, Fédra and I work in tandem. We take phone bookings and talk to people who wander up because their mobiles don't work here and they'd like to make a reservation in person. Some people just come to take a look and see what we're about. I do enjoy talking to them about our menu and telling them that the husband brings in the fresh seafood every afternoon.

Our days in the kitchen are often punctuated by strange occurrences. At Ninth Wave our average day is not very average. We spend a lot of time laughing our way through the day, which is my preferred method. I would rather get up two hours earlier so everything is ahead of schedule and we can enjoy our work.

One day in the summer Jonny brought in an overflowing basket of newly dug potatoes. While cooking some off for use in lobster salad Fédra came across a weird one. She had put it in the pot without noticing it. It was a mutant potato with attitude and we immediately took to him. It seemed quite natural to sit him on the table, make a hat for him out of kitchen labels and set him against a backdrop of a ship in a bottle. I think we must have had some spare time that day! We took a photo of him and put him on Facebook. The listing read 'This sea-faring potato was discovered in our garden today. Because of his hermaphroditic nature (and his propensity for cross-dressing)

we have named him Soltzy Retzso after a curious, quasi-fictional and perhaps somewhat dubious Hungarian singer. Because Soltzy and his potato head have been cooked we felt it only fitting that he be immortalised in this fashion.'

Our Facebook viewer numbers soared and we had ten times the number of likes on our page than usual. It seemed Soltzy was an overnight sensation.

Living and working on a Hebridean island has its drawbacks. Deliveries on Mull are often hindered by cancelled ferries, weather-dependent pursuits such as scallop-diving, or other island oddities. I have had to change the menu an hour before service because quail or lamb racks haven't turned up in time. Depending on how much is left on the list, Fédra goes off at 3 or 4 pm and comes back at 7 pm for dinner service. I forge ahead finishing things up, printing off the menus, putting the menus in their covers, and getting Jonny's dinner ready for him for 6 o'clock. A thousand last-minute things get done between 4 and 6, but it is then that I get a sit-down if possible, while Jonny pops into the bath (not a phone box) to do a Clark Kent, changing from oilskins and fishing gear to the kilt, sporran and garter flashes. At 6, I serve the husband his well-earned dinner and start service set-up in the kitchen.

Hot table on, check. Plates polished, check. Last minute sauces finished, check. Heat lamp on the pass, check. After his meal Jonny turns his hot water urn on, restocks his fridges, reads the menu and does a final check on the tables. In the kitchen I read through the menu and make sure I have every item prepared to my satisfaction. Before I know it, Fédra, and whoever's helping waitress for a few hours, come through the door. It is a time filled with anticipation. Jonny sings out 'It's showtime!' The restaurant lights are turned on, the double glass doors are opened and away we go. I pop outside just before service to pick fresh garnishes such as woodruff, marigolds, sweet peas and nasturtiums for the plates. I often meet the first guests as they arrive while I'm foraging near the parking lot, and get a chance to say hello which is great. At least they know everything's as fresh as can be.

JONNY WELCOMES THE FIRST GUESTS OF THE EVENING

There are mishaps that occur from time to time. The challenge is not letting the event cloud the rest of our day, or indeed the diners' experience. Once the kitchen timer had failed to go off. I went to turn on the oven at 6 to bake some Mull cheddar tuilles for the blinis. Mysteriously, it was already on. I should have smelled something but for some reason hadn't noticed. 'Flooby!' I yelled. He'd been baking all afternoon, and was looking like he'd been on vacation in Namibia. We were an hour away from opening and we had no bread. Faster than I'd ever done, I made another batch in the mixer and put it in the still warm oven to prove. Flooby usually gets a double proving which takes at least two and a half hours, but I only had an hour and a quarter. I made the loaves directly onto the metal sheet tray, portioning them so they were a bit smaller than usual and would bake quickly. I willed him to rise. The bread gods were with me and Flooby did his thing. We only missed the first booking slot by a couple of minutes and Flooby was delivered to the table by a smiling Jonny when the diners were only halfway through their soup. Hot bread straight from the oven. A close call.

During Fédra's first week we were into dinner service and I was training her how to present a half lobster, which is a constant feature on our menu. I was explaining that it must only be cooked for a scant seven minutes and that the utmost care must be taken when preparing the lobster for the plate. I showed her how to half it properly using a sharp knife. Next I explained about the necessity of removing the beast's intestinal tract. I tried to use simple words, as Fédra had just got here from Hungary and I didn't think 'intestinal tract' would have been taught in conversational English classes. I said 'You have to remove the poop from the lobster.' Fédra looked at me perplexed and said very loudly, 'Poop, poop? I do not know thees poop!'

That sent me into a tailspin of laughter from which I never really recovered that night. I showed her the intestine on the lobster and explained that was where the digested food of the lobster went. Fédra's face suddenly brightened up, she smiled and firmly stated, 'Ooh, you mean SHEET!' That night of laughter broke down all the language barriers and we've been great friends ever since.

Our dinner bookings are precisely co-ordinated as we are so small that we run mostly on a skeleton staff. If we have twelve or fewer diners booked for an evening Jonny does the dining room himself. This includes hosting, making cocktails, taking orders, table service, writing bills (yes, Jonny still prefers to write them by hand instead of using 'those infernal machines') and making sure our guests are happy.

People have no idea how being late or early can affect the whole flow of service in such a wee place. Groups of hunting parties and film crews are notorious for being so late that we think twice about taking bookings from them, but we do try our best to be hospitable. Often visitors are unsure of travel times on the island and arrive before our doors are even open. I try not to look alarmed, though our schedule is often timed down to the minute. Sometimes we kindly point them in the direction of the lovely short jaunt to the quarry that has a great view, or we seat them in the foyer to wait for Jonny to finish donning his duds and see them to their table. A couple of times people have come so early that Jonny is still eating his dinner and has to wait until almost midnight to finish it. Such harsh treatment after a hard day's fishing, poor guy.

The Michelin Man

It was early July in our second year, when a friendly couple came to book a table for dinner. They found me in the front garden planting some tree lilies by the pink granite obelisk.

They introduced themselves as the Allans, and told me they'd been visiting Mull for many years and were delighted to hear of the new restaurant. Avid foodies, Robert and Anne-Marie were to become two of our favourite regulars. Leaning on the entrance rail I explained about John catching the lobsters fresh each day. I also mentioned that we were quite busy for our location, but we needed some press and were disappointed not to have had any restaurant reviewers or foodie inspectors visit us. They assured me that recognition would happen in time, booked in for that evening and I waved them off with trowel in hand.

That night we unusually only had two tables booked in, the Allans and a man booked in simply as Gregory. This gave John and I time to chat to both tables.

During the meal Gregory had got up to look at the photos of John and his boat in the foyer. As Anne-Marie was passing him on the way to the Ladies, she heard him say 'Amazing! This is amazing.' She stopped and looked at the photos and said, 'Yes, they are very good photos.' And he answered 'Oh, not the photos, the place. I just can't believe a place this wonderful exists way out here.' Gregory went on to say that he had sampled more than 120 meals that year and only two were memorable. One of the two was the Ninth Wave!

Later I brought the chocolates out and talked to both tables, describing the flavours of my after-dinner chocolates. Both Gregory and the Allans especially enjoyed the raspberry cranachan chocolates.

I was clearing up the kitchen, getting ready to start on planning the next day's menu when in walked John with Gregory. Gregory introduced himself as a Michelin inspector and talked about how much he enjoyed his dining experience. Ambience, genuine friendliness and a lobster course that was in his top two lobster meals ever were his favourite things about the evening. He revelled in the fact that I hadn't over-complicated dishes just for the sake of it and let the seafood speak for itself. He also said that there were great combinations on the menu he'd never seen before. Not wacky or trendy, just imaginative. This is not surprising, since I am a self-taught chef living and working in a virtual culinary vacuum, and our dishes come straight out of my head. I am surely influenced by my chef-ing past in that great melting pot that is Canada, but I adhere to a rule of 'If everyone else is doing it, I don't need to.'

We've now have a two couverts rating in the Michelin guide for the last five years which is great, but I really wish they'd visit again because we have improved greatly in the meantime. I was told that Michelin try to inspect restaurants every six months to a year. Even allowing for our location, I feel one rating in six years isn't quite fair. I like to think we could now achieve the maximum amount of four couverts ratings. Alas, I doubt if we'd ever be considered for a star as we just don't meet certain criteria. Our food certainly tastes as good as some 1, 2 or even 3-star Michelin restaurants, so some of our diners tell us. Where we differ is the service. Attentive, unique and genuine it is, but we miss out some of the more traditional points of 'fine dining' (a term we are careful to avoid). Although the food is of very high quality, served with imagination and aplomb, we lack some of the finer graces. After all, John is a fisherman and I am but a colonial. On his own most nights, John doesn't have the time (or quite frankly the desire) to ponce around brandishing corkscrews at the table or fiddling with silver service. It is this mixture of top-notch ideals and informality that seems to appeal to a lot of our guests. This being said, we do strive continually to better ourselves, our produce and our service.

Sour grapes aside, I am quite grateful never to have to play the star rating game as I think the stress involved to keep it up would be pretty rough. As it is, I often have to scrape the old grey matter off the kitchen ceiling after juggling the garden, the ordering, the foraging, the cooking and the laundry issues.

On Mull the question we get asked the most often is, 'What do you do in the winter?' Some people like fishermen, crofters, grocers, mechanics and council employees work all year round as in most places. The seasonal nature of our tourism industry on Mull does mean, however, that a lot of businesses close or cut their opening hours from November to Easter. Winter gives those of us who do, a chance to socialise and have a bit of a life, since work is pretty full-on during the season. And I get to sleep in.

It is easy here for winter hibernation mode to set in. We all want to sleep more and are beset by cravings for mounds of mince and tatties or crumble and custard. The days are very short and dark and it gets harder to motivate yourself. But needs must. Winter at Ninth Wave is the only time I have for trying out new foods, dishes and preserving methods. I tried out some new chutneys before Christmas last year and am about to dip my foot into the weird waters of molecular spherification.

I also use the time to catch up on marketing and reassess internet listings and our website. Adverts, brochures and the face of Ninth Wave have to be updated and refreshed each year, and as I design and write them all, it's quite time-consuming. Any dental, medical or hair appointments (in Oban) must be arranged for our closed period as we don't usually get off the island from May to September. And in winter we have friends over for dinner parties. I force Jonny to play charades.

STORM CLOUD OVER IONA

JONNY FISHING

This November and February, we opened for speciality lunches and brunches on the odd weekend and also hosted trivia quiz nights to keep the grey matter lively. What else? I go out for coffee with friends and catch up on what's happened over the season. I avidly read books by our wood-burning stove in my red flannel pyjamas and have gone through a dozen food memoirs and over fifty novels this winter. I go to the mobile movie theatre called 'The Scream Machine' which lands in Craignure every month. Crafts, biscuits, caramels and chocolates are made to sell at the Christmas fairs which take place from late November until mid December and that keeps me busy for a whole month. It is in the off-season too that I go on courses and master-classes to keep my culinary skills sharp; it was a chocolate master-class at Cocoa Blacks this year.

Jonny still goes fishing as usual every day if the weather is fit, but at least he gets the evenings to relax. He can be found at the village pub from 6 until 7 pm most days, enjoying his pre-prandial pint of 80-shilling. His winter gardening tasks include clearing dead plant matter, fertilising with seaweed from beach, turning over the garden, repairing fencing and indoor seed cultivation. He goes logging and cuts all the wood for our wood-burner on the days that it's too bad to fish.

The highlight of our yearly social calendar is our Halloween Steampunk Party. Fifty or so friends, B&B owners and patrons of the restaurant don alter-egos and dress in neo-Victorian costume. It is a time to celebrate the end of another great season with food and drink and explore the wonders of mechanical magic.

Here is an article about the event that I wrote for the local paper *Round and About Mull and Iona*. It gives you a good idea what some of us really get up to here on Mull.

Temporal Voyagers Steampunk Symposium

The Steampunk Symposium at Ninth Wave near Fionnphort, Mull on October 31st was deemed an outrageous success.

After cleaning up the last of the cosmic dust, Kyper Belt debris and Test Tube cocktail remains and closing a fracture in the time/steam space continuum I, Dr Anoushka Marmoleum can honestly say that monumental effort went into Steampunk fashion statements across the board and the plethora of perfectly pandemoniacal hats. Never have so many leather corsets and top hats been seen on Mull!

Months of planning by all parties involved led to the largest display of Steampunkery ever exhibited in the Hebrides. The Whimshurst Contrivance was built and showcased by Dr Erasmus Brasspounder himself. Many couples availed themselves of the opportunity to receive *'Electric Kisses'* from the machine. A few corpses which had imbibed too many 'Persephone's Underworld' and 'Mr Renfield' cocktails were apparently resuscitated by the experiment.

Lady Absynthe and Reptilius Aasvogel's Weaponry, on display in the South Wing, was admired from a distance and the crowd was enthralled by Grizelda's skeletal specimen coat. Dr Ottenbaum helped assemble the Glycol Orb Machine (giant bubble-maker) and encouraged the audience to chant the ominous words Oooomla-ooomla to invoke the appropriate Flaggis Goddess of Orbs.

The Contessa Dell' Oscuro was on hand to sign copies of her much acclaimed new book *Through Underground Nepal with Lamp and Vasculum*.

Other highlights included Alberta Beeching's Steam-powered Lepidoptera Sculpture and Cogsnipe's Forehead Sextant.

Several incidents threaten to disturb the demonstrations including spillage from the Glycol Orb, but that was soon swabbed-up by Squadron Leader Dreadnought and his nifty swiffer. Hepzibah Megatron lost a

AT THE STEAMPUNK SYMPOSIUM

cog swail and Baron Cyn Scarlet completely vanished, last seen eating a chicken wing by the psychic telephone in questionable company.

A full house of freaky-fraternity Steamers was buzzing until the unitary clock went into overtime. Rocket carriages and Steam Limousines whirled away into the aether at 1 am British Empire Time, as Jonny Dreadnought and Anoushka waved them a bleary farewell.

We take our wee foodie tours in February or March when the weather is foul and the fishing is slow. The last two years' adventures were in Morocco and Baja Mexico. It's amazing what a bit of sun does for the spirit. We recharge our batteries and come back ready to get the restaurant, the road, garden and croft in shape for opening.

So when asked 'What do you do in the winter?' I usually just say, 'A lot!'

Me and My Food

As chef of Ninth Wave another question I am often asked is, 'Where do you get your inspiration from?'

There are a thousand answers to this question.

My background is central to my inspiration. As with most chefs, food played a great part in my upbringing. My mom made huge feasts of Chinese food in the 1960s Canadian prairies when it was unheard of to cook it at home (unless you were Chinese of course). Every Sunday all of us would beg, barter and steal for the privilege of bringing home friends to share my mom's famous dinners. My mom, 'Babe' (so named as the youngest in her family) was born in the Canadian prairies of Saskatchewan to parents of French descent. My grandmother was orphaned at an early age and went to work in a hotel kitchen at the age of 11 to support her younger siblings. That hotel flair rubbed off on her cooking, and in turn my mother was very into food and presented each plate of dinner with artistry and verve. No matter what else was happening in our house of five kids, the dinners were a sanctuary of blissful flavours.

Even after I moved out of the house, when visiting my mom the first thing she'd say was, 'Hi there, you! What do you feel like eating?'

There are fragmented moments out of time that influence how I feel about food. Every time I crimp the edge of a pastry shell I can see and feel my mother's hands crimping a hundred pies before me. She's gone now, but would have revelled in the hedonism that is Ninth Wave. I still use her old rolling pin that was carved out of a single block of Canadian maple and was a wedding present in 1940. All the pastries I make here are imbued with these positive connections.

My first experience of a restaurant kitchen was when I was fourteen. In career education class we'd been asked to pick a place we'd like to do a work experience stint at for a week. For the first one I picked a garage (I wanted to be a mechanic that week) and for the second a cool two-storey restaurant called Noo's Pizza. It had a jazz stage that could be seen from both floors, a viewing window into the kitchen and the only wholewheat pizzas in Victoria. I stayed there working the summers and weekends for a couple years. There I learned the art of tossing a round of pizza dough 20 feet in the air to ring a bell that hung on the ceiling. Actually, I never really got the hang of it and my toss exhibited, instead, a tendency towards a horizontal trajectory straight into the kitchen wall.

In later years I have of course absorbed the influences of famous chefs, TV programmes, and the world of food blogs on the internet. Another major inspiration is the food that Jonny and I discover on our winter travels. Each February, when the relentless rain and gales have driven us shack-wacky, we look for solace in a spot of sun. We've eaten chilli-laden Tom Yum Kung from street sellers in Bangkok, which is where my recipe for Thai won ton soup evolved from. We have dived into steaming bowls of peanutty Massaman curry on a tiny island in the Andaman Sea, which is where the recipe for my Venison Fillet in Massaman Sauce and Garden Tatties began life. We have devoured char-grilled lamb, cooked on handmade barbecues in straggling markets on the edge of the Sahara desert, which now influences the flavours I pair with local Scottish lamb. We have braved the smoky, noisy sensory overload that is Place Jemaa el Fnaa in the heart of Marrakesh to eat spicy homemade sausages, which has made me change the way I make my chorizo. We've quaffed bags full of fiery potato and coconut rotis from stands on the beaches of Southern Sri Lanka, and eaten Egyptian packed lunches while gazing at the great pyramids in the noonday heat. We've breakfasted on Canadian maple-cured bacon on a warm stack of pancakes while rolling through the Rocky Mountains on a train, and lunched on homemade three bean soup in an un-named living room restaurant in the back lanes of a Cypriot village. All of these experiences reside in my chef's brain, silently guiding my hands as I work in my kitchen on the quiet coast of a Scottish isle.

My creative processes vary when it comes to food. I can sit with paper and design dishes like a culinary architect, but they often lack heart and aren't the best examples of my work. Many of my dishes have slowly evolved over time. Here is an example.

For my birthdays I always asked my eldest brother Ron to cook his Greek food for me. He'd been to Mykanos on his first vacation abroad and he'd spent a lot of time recreating the dishes he'd had there. My favourite was Spanakopita, which is a layered pie made with spinach, onions, dill, feta and filo pastry. Later in my twenties I asked for the recipe and made it for the staff when I worked at the hotel on Iona. In later years I added a bit of cream and some basil. When running my catering business I thought that the deconstructed filling and filo pastry would make good accompaniments to plump Inverlussa mussels. Then I omitted the filo and feta as it seemed a bit 80s, and decided to add the liquorice taste of Pernod to the creamed spinach mix. When I opened the restaurant I used garden chard, added turmeric, made a lighter mix with less cream and paired it with hand-dived scallops. Today you will often find Scallops with Pernod Chard on the menu with the addition of crispy Argyll smoked ham and two caviars.

I sometimes create a dish solely from the starting point of the garden harvest. We grow a lot of beetroot and horseradish in the garden, they seem

to like the weather here. We grow Burpee's Golden, red Rubidus and white and purple striped Chioggia beetroot. I wanted to make them the star of their own dish. I know beetroot figures quite prominently in Russian cuisine. There was a Russian lady who lived on our block when I was a kid and used to feed me great blinis. I remembered the toasty taste of the buckwheat flour and how fluffy they were. I thought I would combine the two. Our blinis with a trio of sweet, earthy beetroot was born, and sour cream with sharp garden horseradish melded the elements together. I often add grated Inverloch goat's cheese to the sour cream when it's in season, or pair the blini stack with a cumin and avocado bavarois in the summer. Our Sorrel Linguini with Broad beans, Peas and Land Cress is another one of these garden-inspired dishes.

The dictionary definition of inspiration is *a drawing in of breath*, and indeed I do create from everything I breathe in from the magical world around me.

THAI MULL LOBSTER AND CRAB WONTON SOUP

This zingy soup is a favourite with our customers. Its sweet, salty, sour and hot tastes are balanced to complement the fresh seafood.

Serves 4

RED THAI PASTE
3 shallots, diced
15g/½oz lemongrass paste
1 chilli, diced
5 garlic cloves
15g/½oz galangal
15g/½oz fish sauce
15g/½oz palm sugar
5 kaffir lime leaves, powdered
5g/¼oz turmeric
45g/1½oz fresh coriander

SOUP
½ tsp of vegetable oil
45ml/1½fl oz red Thai curry paste
580ml/20fl oz water
165g/6oz tin of water chestnuts
    (save 4 for wonton filling)
water from water chestnuts
15g/½oz palm sugar
60ml/2fl oz fish sauce
1 tin coconut milk
1 spring onion, sliced
1 chilli thinly sliced
1 lime, juiced

WONTONS
1 package wonton wrappers

FILLING
170g/6oz white crab meat (drained)
170g/6oz lobster meat
2 tsp Thai red curry paste
pinch sea salt
1 tsp spring onion, finely chopped
4 water chestnuts, finely diced

FOR RED THAI CURRY PASTE, puree all ingredients for two minutes in a processor. Any extra paste will keep in the fridge up to three weeks in an airtight container and can be used for curries or to marinate meat.

FOR SOUP, heat oil in a pot on low heat. Sauté the red Thai curry paste for five minutes while stirring.

Add water, chestnuts, chestnut water and sugar to the pot, stirring all the paste into the liquid. Heat to boiling. Add fish sauce and coconut milk. Heat until steaming and almost boiling, while whisking in the solids of the coconut cream.

Add lime juice and mix. When re-heating do not boil, as the coconut oil will separate out and float on the top of the soup.

FOR WONTON FILLING, squeeze excess water out of the crab or leave in a strainer for 10 minutes to drain. Mix all ingredients except water chestnuts in a food processor on pulse setting just until mixed into a ball. Stir in the water chestnuts by hand.

FOR WONTONS, place a wonton wrapper on a cutting board, keeping the rest wrapped well to avoid drying. Brush the edges with water and then place a rounded teaspoon of filling in the middle. Diagonally fold the edges together to make a triangle, ensuring that no mixture gets between the edges. Crimp with your fingers to seal completely. Set finished wontons aside on a tray finely sprinkled with cornflour. Repeat until filling is all used. This recipe usually makes 24 wontons.

Just before you are ready to serve the soup, boil a large pan of salted water. Add the wontons to the boiling water and stir gently with a wooden spoon, making sure the dough doesn't stick to the bottom or sides of the pan. Boil for two minutes and transfer the wontons using a slotted spoon into warm serving bowls before pouring in the heated soup. Garnish with spring onion, fresh coriander or fresh chillies.

SOUND OF IONA LANGOUSTINES WITH MANGO AND COINTREAU DRESSING

I think langoustines have a sweeter and creamier flesh than that of a lobster. If you are adventurous, you can serve these beauties whole and spend some leisure time slowly teasing the meat out of the tails and claws, or you can peel them beforehand.

Serves 4

28 large langoustines, cooked, tailed and peeled
4 whole for presentation
125g/4oz mixed washed garden greens, such as lamb's lettuce, mibuna, little gem lettuce and cress
2 sprigs tarragon, chopped
2 sprigs dill, chopped
6 large sorrel leaves, chopped
8 mange touts, sliced thinly
1 small mango, peeled and sliced

COINTREAU DRESSING
1 small orange, peeled, pith removed and sectioned
50g/2oz mayonnaise
50g/2oz crème fraiche
2 tsp Cointreau liqueur
½ tsp white wine vinegar
pinch celery salt
dash nam pla fish sauce

Boil the whole langoustines in a large pot of salted water for three minutes or until the meat on the underside of the tail is white and no longer translucent. Drain and cool quickly on a tray. They can be eaten straight away, or chilled for a cold salad, or peeled as you wish. If peeling them, I usually save one whole to garnish each plate. Please see the information panel on 'How to Peel Langoustines, Prawns etc'.

To make the Cointreau dressing, whisk all ingredients together until smooth. Season to taste.

Mix the selection of greens with the tarragon, dill, sorrel and mange touts.

To serve, divide the mango slices between four plates or cocktail glasses and fan them, if you are adventurous. Serve the prawns on the salad with a good dollop of the cointreau dressing. Garnish with cress.

HOW TO PEEL LANGOUSTINES, PRAWNS ETC.

To peel langoustines, start by twisting the tail away from the head and claws. There are sharp barbs on the underside of the langoustine so you might wish to wear kitchen gloves. The tail shell is comprised of six segments. Hold the sides of the tail between each of your thumbs and forefingers, with your fingers pointing towards each other. Move the tail carefully back and forth sideways (the tail forming a U-shape) to break the shell on both sides between the third and fourth segments. Turn the langoustines belly-up, and between a finger and thumb pinch the base of the tail firmly. With the other thumb and forefinger, gently grasp the exposed meat between the segments while gently teasing the meat out. This should allow you to remove the tail in one piece. If the prawns are peeled raw this pinching of the tail will also tend to remove the dark intestinal tract which is essential.

DARK CHOCOLATE AND BRAMBLE TART

This luscious tart appears on the restaurant menu in different guises depending on the season. Here it is paired with fresh picked berries and whin-infused cream.

Serves 6

THE TART
270g/9oz Valrhona Araguani dark
   chocolate callettes (chips)
65g/2oz butter, diced
315ml/15fl oz double cream
3 egg yolks
Follow recipe of chocolatine biscuit
   dough for base, see page 79

THE BRAMBLE PUREE
170g/6oz brambles, washed
1 tbsp vanilla caster sugar
pinch salt
40 more brambles for presentation
   (10 per person)

First place the washed whin flowers in the cream and infuse, covered, in the fridge for 4-12 hours. If you are substituting coconut liqueur for the blossoms then you can skip this stage. Strain the blossoms, then whip the cream and sugar and vanilla seeds together until soft peaks form. Chill in the fridge until ready to assemble the tart.

Preheat the oven to 180C/160C fan/350F/Gas 4. Take a fluted tart dish with a removable bottom. I use a 35 x 11cm rectangular aluminium dish. Grease and flour your fluted tin well, knocking it gently upside-down to remove any excess flour.

WHIN BLOSSOM CREAM
160ml/5½fl oz double cream
large handful whin blossoms
    (177ml) or 1 tsp coconut liqueur
1 tsp sieved icing sugar
¼ vanilla pod seeds

Make the chocolatine dough as instructed on page 79. Roll it out on a floured silicone baking sheet until 4mm thick and a shape and size to line your tart tin. Place a silicone or greaseproof sheet over the pastry and fill with baking beans or the equivalent to blind bake the pastry case. Bake on a tray for 12 minutes, then remove the beans and paper. Bake for 10 minutes uncovered, then trim excess pastry off the edges while still hot.

FOR THE TART FILLING, preheat the oven to 160C/140C fan/325F/Gas 3. Put the chocolate and butter in a bowl. Heat the cream to almost boiling and pour over the chocolate and butter. Stir until smooth. Stir in the beaten egg yolks.

Pour into the tart case until 0.5cm from the top. Refrigerate extra filling in an airtight container (this will be used as a crème chocolat). Bake the tart for 25 minutes until small bubbles begin to appear on the tart surface, and when wiggled, only the middle still wobbles. Cool to room temperature and then chill. When chilled remove the tart from the tin, portion and trim as desired.

TO MAKE BRAMBLE PUREE, blend the berries and sugar in a processor. Strain through a fine sieve and discard the seeds. This can be made several days ahead and chilled.

To serve, spoon some of the bramble puree onto the plate. Place a slice of tart on each plate. Place eight brambles on top of each piece of tart. Pipe the whin cream between the brambles to add a decorative touch. Pipe a whorl of cream onto the plate and top with two brambles. Place a quenelle of the crème chocolat tart filling that you kept aside in the fridge on one side of the tart. The tart can then be garnished with your choice of chocolate decoration. (In the picture, we have garnished the tart plate with a dollop of bramble ice cream sandwiched between two chocolatine biscuits.)

MOCHATINE BISCUITS

Chocolatines★ were the original Oreo cookies. Crunchy, chocolatey and very moreish, this is a modern take on a French classic with the addition of coffee. I use these to make our mini ice-cream sandwiches and to decorate desserts.

Makes 3 dozen

30g/1oz sifted plain flour
180g/6½oz organic cocoa
1¼ tsp baking powder
1/8 tsp salt
300g/10oz vanilla caster sugar
180g/6½oz butter, soft
¾ tsp instant coffee
1 tsp boiling water
1 tsp brandy
1 large egg
roasted coffee beans for garnishing

Preheat the oven to 200C/180C fan/400F/Gas 6. Dissolve the coffee in a teaspoon of boiling water.

In a large bowl, beat the sugar and butter together. Beat in the brandy, cooled coffee and egg. Sift the flour, cocoa, baking powder and salt together onto the wet mixture in the bowl. Mix well with a wooden spoon or with your hands. Chill the dough, covered, for 10 minutes.

Place a silicone baking sheet on a flat surface and coat lightly with flour. Place the dough on this sheet. Sprinkle the dough with flour. Roll out with a lightly floured rolling pin until 3mm thick. Dust off any remaining flour from the top with a soft, damp (not wet) cloth. Cut with a round (or other) cookie cutter. Place on a tray lined with a silicone baking sheet 3cm apart and bake for 8-10 minutes or until firm in the middle. Decorate with a coffee bean.

★for chocolatines just leave out the coffee elements

CARDAMOM STARS

At Ninth Wave you'll find these crunchy spiced biscuits on top of our ice creams and panna cottas. We can often be found dunking them in a cup of tea at elevenses.

Makes 3 dozen

115g/4oz self-raising flour
½ tsp bicarbonate of soda
½ tsp baking powder
50g/2oz vanilla caster sugar
50g/2oz margarine
1 tbsp golden syrup
½ tsp ground cardamom
pinch ground ginger

Preheat the oven to 190C/170C fan/375F/Gas 5.

Sift the flour, spices, bicarbonate of soda and baking powder together into a medium bowl. Add the sugar and mix well. With your fingertips, rub the margarine into the dry ingredients until it resembles fine crumbs. Add syrup and mix in well. The mixture should be silky and not sticky. If too wet, add a touch more flour and knead.

Place a silicone baking sheet on a flat surface and coat lightly with flour. Place dough on the sheet and sprinkle with flour. Roll out with a floured rolling pin until 3mm thick. Cut with a star (or other) cookie-cutter. Place on a greased baking tray 3cm apart and bake for 10 minutes or until golden brown and firm in the middle. Keep a close watch as they only take a minute or so to over-bake and every oven's temperatures vary. Remove from the oven. Wait 5 minutes and then place the biscuits onto a wire rack to cool.

WHITE PEONY SHORTBREAD

Sweet Chinese white peony tea is a perfect addition to our traditional Scottish shortbread. You can also try using any loose leaf tea such as Assam, Earl Grey or even powdered matcha tea. These shortbreads are very addictive and never last very long around here. I also use them to decorate desserts.

Makes 3 dozen

100g/4oz butter, softened
25g/1oz corn flour
125g/5oz plain flour
15g/½oz loose leaf tea
pinch salt
65g/2½oz vanilla caster sugar

Preheat oven to 150C/130C fan/300F/Gas 2.

Cream the sugar and butter until well mixed. Sift the flours and salt together into a medium bowl. Add the tea. Using your fingertips, rub the room temperature butter into the dry ingredients until incorporated and bring the dough together into a ball. If the mix is too dry, add a small dot more of butter and mix with your hands until the dough is smooth and silky.

Place a silicone baking sheet on a flat surface and coat lightly with flour. Place the dough on the sheet sprinkle with flour and roll out with floured rolling pin until 5mm thick. Cut with a 4cm square (or other) cookie-cutter. Place on a greased baking tray 3cm apart and bake for 30 minutes, or until golden brown and firm in the middle.

Remove from the oven. Wait 5 minutes and then place the biscuits onto a wire rack to cool.

 TO THE BOAT AND BACK

When the wind's in the north,
The good fisher goes not forth,
When the wind's in the east,
He catches the least,
When the wind's in the south,
He feeds many a mouth,
And when the wind's in the west,
The fishing's the best.

Anon

Bucket on arm, Jonny starts his daily early morning journey to his boat, the *Sonsie*. Her name is a Scots word meaning handsome, buxom and jolly, and it suits her well. Dressed in his yellow oilskins, Jonny walks up our track and through the upper gate towards the pink tower rock that is Tor Mor. He has had his tankard-sized cup of coffee and his usual fry-up to prepare him for a physically demanding day of fishing. This time of day the quality of light makes the granite outcrops glow with a rosy hue. Soon he is up the hill at the disused quarry that supplied much of the stone for the Iona nunnery and abbey as well as nearby Skerryvore Lighthouse, built by the famous Stevenson dynasty of lighthouse-builders in the mid-1800s.

As he goes along, he nimbly steps on and over the giant blocks of cut Caledonian granite, jumbled like a megalithic game of Jenga, to get down to and across a boggy moor. On automatic pilot Jonny strides his way around peat bogs on a barely-discernible path used only by sheep. Watching for

JONNY AND THE *SONSIE*

hares, and otters heading back towards the ocean, he forges ahead in the dawn light. Without warning a bundle of squawking feathers launches itself out of the tussocky grass at his feet and gives rise to one of his 'OOH, YA BUGGER, YA!' moments. The brown-spotted snipe pips with indignation at being disturbed, but I think she secretly enjoys giving Jonny a fright. Another twenty minutes and the entrance to a cleft in the rocks swings into view to the west.

The way continues down this steep gully to Bull Hole, where both the Fionnphort fishing fleet and the Calmac ferry are moored. Most days the greeting committee is a pair of ravens that nest in the cliff face just above the moorings. Their deep 'gronking' sound reverberates off the steep rocks, creating an otherworldly effect. To Jonny the ravens are always a welcome sight, and a symbol of fidelity as they mate for life. Keeping as fit as ever (he's over 60) John rows out to the *Sonsie* in all weathers. The *Sonsie* is a 20-foot fibreglass version of its predecessor. His old boat, the beloved clinker-built *Helga* was a lovely all-wooden craft that was built in the 60s in Wales to ferry cattle to and from islands. After 50 years of repairs it performed more like a sieve than a boat and was sadly retired in 2009. We had a village barbecue in honour of the event and burnt the *Helga* in a Viking-like funeral ceremony on the croft.

Once aboard the boat, he performs the daily equipment tests, stores the bait fish, fills up with diesel and heads out to haul creels. Every once in a while Jonny's day is livened-up by a strange find in the creels. Among the strangest were a bright red lobster, a family of wee purple sea slugs, a sea mouse and a drowned mink. After 30 years of fishing these turquoise waters John still loves and lives to catch lobster. He never tires of seeing the elusive bright blue lobsters in the traps, and working amidst the breathtaking beauty of the islands.

One day while fishing the south side of the Ross of Mull at Shiaba, John was engrossed in watching the creels coming up in the hauler. Just as he spotted a good-size lobster, a massive 'Whoosh!' exploded just behind him and a spout of foul-smelling spray landed on his head. He was so startled he dropped the creel.

A smooth, dark grey body with a blow hole was disappearing under the sea as he turned to look. A minke whale. It was the length of a bus. Stopping the hauler, John sat down and waited for another sight of this noble beast. After ten minutes of hopefully watching the surface, he gave up and went back to the creels. As he hauled up the first one, another 'Whoosh!' detonated only yards away. Shouting 'By Jesus!' he dropped the creel. The minke whale saluted goodbye with another spout of water as he made his way back out of the bay, an encounter which prompted Jonny to say 'Bonnie beasts, but they really have bad breath, do the whales!'

Dabberlocks and Bladderwrack

Early January. Jonny and I had finally surfaced from the usual whisky haze of a Fionnphort Hogmanay. Ideas have now begun to burble through the bog of my culinary mind and out into the watery daylight of a Hebridean winter.

I decided that my first experiment this year was to make some mystical powders from local edible seaweeds. Gem-coloured sea lettuce and dusky dulse to start with.

I occasionally ask Jonny to collect seaweed for me when he is on the way to the *Sonsie*. He searches among the mooring lines, rocks and shore near his boat for the many different varieties which I use in our kitchen. These include oarweed, sea lettuce, bladderwrack and other seaweeds. Sea lettuce obligingly clings to the anchor ropes of the lobster keeps or washes up on the white sands of nearby Tor Mor beach, looking like transparent emerald shards from a stained glass window. Bladderwrack can be gathered by the armful on most shores here, especially after a gale, and John finds purple dulse in the tiny, raven-guarded cove where his battered dinghy is kept. There are endless ways to use this wonderful resource. With their high iodine content and saltiness, sea plants add a wonderful element to scallops, crab or fish dishes.

The experiment begins. In the kitchen, I am up to my oxters in drying seaweed. It is a game of patience and requires perfect relative humidity. Pots boiling on the stove seem to rehydrate the seaweed, leaving their skeins flaccid and unappealing (oh dear) and the process has to begin again.

I was determined to have fun. I put on an Alice Cooper CD and dove into the project with gay abandon.

On several forays into the kitchen Jonny had mistaken me for the *Creature from the Black Lagoon*, and quickly retreated to the comparative safety of his boat during a gale force 8 storm. Perhaps the flannel pyjamas/wet suit combo with welding goggles wasn't my best look.

All week long friends from the Ross of Mull stopped by for coffee or a chat, only to find that they were required to navigate a maze of submarine botanicals hanging from every available fixture and festooning every appliance. Some were too timid and left before they even got to the kitchen. Perhaps '*Welcome to My Nightmare!*' booming from the speakers was a contributing factor? I think some poor souls went missing for several days, only to stumble across me eventually, wading knee deep in kelp, wearing scuba gear and screeching 'up the yardarm . . . set the mainsails . . . yo ho ho and a bottle of Ledaig!' Even the seafaring Jonny donned his sou'wester in the kitchen and kept me at arm's length with his impressively large boathook.

I dried four types of seaweed in all – bladderwrack, kelp, sea lettuce and purple dulse. I rinsed, drained, strained, splattered, plattered, sliced and diced.

As I did so, I thought of St Columba and his monks on nearby Iona who are credited with writing the oldest recorded account of seaweed as a food in Great Britain. The sixth century monks were said to collect seaweeds in their hoisted-up habits, with their knobbly knees on show, for both themselves and the poor. The monks then cooked them in oatmeal, thick broth or simply

SEAWEED AS SEASONING

I use dried and powdered or flaked seaweeds.

Bladderwrack **Fucus vesticulosis** has a bold, fishy and salty taste with a metallic tang. Not for the faint-hearted. I use it in Hebridean Fish Chowder and in Thai cooking as a substitute for fish sauce.

Dabberlocks (Wakame) **Alaria esculenta** has a strong, green spinach flavour, which is lovely in salad dressings, pasta dough and buerre blanc. I add it to blinis and our crab cheesecake.

Dulse (Purple Laver) **Palmaria palmate** is a smoky, intense seasoning that enhances beef, lamb and well-aged game. I dry-rub our venison with it and add it to oatcakes and savoury crumbles.

Oarweed (Kombu) **Laminaria digitata** is brimming with umami. It boasts an earthy taste somewhat like morel mushrooms, adding depth to Duck Wellington or venison cassoulets. Works well with truffle.

Pepper Dulse **Osimundea pinnatifida** is the spiciest of all the seaweeds with a hot, peppery finish. Goes well in curries, mouclade and salsa.

Sea Lettuce (Green Nori) **Ulva lactica** has a fresh and salty, punchy taste. We add it to our daily malthouse bread and make seaweed butter for our sea urchin dishes with it. Very versatile.

boiled them as a vegetable. Cooked dulse was known as *slake* and green sea lettuce, that was eaten much like the Welsh laverbread, was known as *sloccan*.

In later centuries seaweed ash was often used as a preservative for fish in the Western Isles, as salt was scarce and expensive.

I'd always wanted to be a mad scientist. Most of my friends said I'd got the mad part right, and I *did* get to wear a white jacket every day. Since this was an experiment, I had now become that mad scientist. First I tried mixing the seaweeds into Valrhona ganache to see if it was viable as a chocolate flavouring. The results were intriguing. It was very easy to overpower the chocolate, and hard to balance the intensity and salt levels. Using my magic spoonula I was transformed into a whirligig, folding seaweeds into pasta, green tea cake, pasties, pickles and pestos.

I did persevere with trying different combinations and we now serve Seaweed and Hebridean Sea Salt Chocolates, and a gnocchi made with purple dulse and wild ramsons.

The seaweed powders have now been stored. Jonny has breathed a sigh of relief. Our kitchen is once again our own and my scuba outfit has curiously disappeared . . . so friends, if you're passing by, the kettle is on, and it's safe to stop in for a cuppa.

MULL FISH CHOWDER WITH PEPPER DULSE

This chowder is a rich and creamy Canadian recipe and is a great way to use odd scraps of various fish that you may find in the freezer. You can buy great dried seaweed mixes from Mara Seaweed on the internet.

Serves 4

600g/1½lb mixed fish, e.g. hake, haddock, pollock, gurnard, skin and bones removed, and cut into 2cm cubes
1 tbsp butter
5 shallots, peeled and diced
2 carrots, peeled and diced
1 small bulb fennel, about 180g, diced
1 tbsp plain white flour
90ml/3fl oz chardonnay wine
600ml/20fl oz cooled fish stock
½ tsp sumac powder
¼ tsp Worcester sauce
1 bay leaf
1 tsp dried seaweed flakes: dulse, kombu or sea lettuce
350ml/12fl oz double cream
sea salt and crushed black pepper to taste

Heat a large heavy pot over a low heat. Add butter and, stirring constantly, sweat the shallots, fennel and carrots until the onions are translucent.

Add the flour and mix well with a balloon whisk. Continue cooking and stirring over medium heat until the flour/butter mixture has turned a light nutty brown in colour.

Add the wine and cook for a minute, while whisking until all the flour lumps have dissolved.

Add the cold stock, seaweed, sumac, Worcester sauce and the bay leaf. Turn up the heat and bring to the boil while stirring occasionally so that the bottom of the pan does not burn. Turn the heat down and simmer for 8-10 minutes. When the carrots are almost tender, add the fish cubes and season. Cook over a low heat until the fish is done, 2 to 4 minutes. Remove the pot from the heat.

Gently stir in the cream and season again if necessary. Heat gently to scald, not boiling, and serve with nori and flax crackers.

PEPPER DULSE SEAWEED AND FLAX CRACKERS

These nutty tasting crisp crackers last for weeks in an airtight container.
Makes 2-4 dozen

50g/2oz wholemeal flour
100g/4oz white flour
100g/4oz ground almonds
40g/1½oz dry flaked pepper dulse
  seaweed
pinch sea salt
30g/1oz flax seeds
90-100ml/3-3½fl oz water

Preheat the oven to 180C/160C fan/350F/Gas 4.

Mix everything except the water and flax seeds together in a food processor. Add the water and seeds and mix in with a wooden spoon until moist but not wet. Knead the dough for three minutes until smooth. Cover the dough and rest it for ten minutes.

Roll out thinly between two silicone baking sheets until 2-3mm thick. Cut into 5cm diameter circles for crackers and 2cm circles for croutons. Brush lightly with water and sprinkle with sea salt.

Place on a non-stick baking sheet. Bake for 20-30 minutes until crispy.

NINTH WAVE MALTHOUSE LOAF

This is our signature daily bread that we serve with whipped Scottish organic butter. It is moist, flavourful and goes with everything. Malthouse bread flour is made from wheat and rye flours combined with flaked malted grains for a wholesome crunchy texture. Jonny gets the bread in his sandwiches every day and never complains.

Makes 1 loaf

150g/5oz organic malthouse flour
350g/12oz organic strong white
   flour
1 tsp quick yeast
1 tsp sugar
½ tsp sea salt
2 tbsp dried dulse seaweed flakes
40ml/1½fl oz olive oil
333ml/15fl oz warm water
a spray bottle of water

Mix together the flours, salt, half the seaweed flakes and yeast in a large bowl. Make a well in the centre and pour in the warm water and oil. Stir to form a soft dough. Turn the dough out onto a lightly floured surface and knead for 5 to 10 minutes until smooth and elastic. Put in a large greased bowl and cover with plastic wrap. Keep in a warm place until doubled in size (about an hour).

Punch the dough down and shape into an oblong. Place on a greased baking tray and spray the loaf and tray with water. Sprinkle the remaining seaweed flakes over the top. Cover with a large piece of foil, leaving enough air space for the bread to expand and not touch the foil. Put it in a warm place and allow the dough to rise until doubled in size (about 50 minutes).

Preheat the oven to 180C/160C fan/350F/Gas 4.

Bake for 45-55 minutes until the bread is golden brown. It should make a hollow sound when tapped underneath. Remove from the tray and place on a cooling rack.

This bread can be frozen as soon as it is cooled, but is best eaten fresh as it has no preservatives in it.

ULVA OYSTERS WITH GREEN TEA, SAMPHIRE AND SEA LETTUCE

A delicious combination of local, plump oysters, fresh seaweed and baby garden vegetables.

Serves 4

8 fresh shucked oysters, with juices
4 large sprigs chervil
30g/1oz samphire
8 baby carrots, cleaned
12 baby spinach, washed and
    stemmed
60g/2oz julienne of Granny Smith
    apple in lemon water
15g/½oz sea lettuce leaves
merlot sea salt

GREEN TEA DRESSING
1 pinch matcha tea powder
2 tsp hot water
2 tsp Stark rapeseed oil
5 tbsp sour cream
2 tsp agave syrup or honey
4 tsp mandarin juice
1 tsp white wine vinegar
1 tsp apple juice
1 tsp Worcester sauce
pinch sea salt

GREEN TEA VINAIGRETTE
1 pinch matcha tea powder
agave syrup
rapeseed oil
cider vinegar
½ tsp fish sauce
strained juice from the oysters
salt
sichuan pepper, ground

Make each of the dressings by whisking the ingredients together and seasoning to taste.

Blanch the carrots in boiling salted water until they are just tender: 3–6 minutes depending on size. Blanch the samphire in boiling unsalted water for 20 seconds and drain on a paper towel. Blanch seaweed in unsalted boiling water for one second.

Place the shucked oysters in the green tea vinaigrette two minutes before serving.

Cut fine matchsticks of Granny Smith apple and cover them with water that has half a lemon squeezed into it. This will keep them from turning brown.

In serving plates or bowls, place the baby spinach, carrots and sea lettuce. Place the drained oysters on the plate. Top the oysters with a drop of green tea sour cream dressing and some apple sticks. Garnish with sea lettuce, chervil sprigs and merlot sea salt.

95

Seafood in Mull Waters

The waters surrounding Mull are cold and nutrient-rich, thanks to the Gulf Stream. This provides some of the best breeding grounds for seafood in the world. As well as fishing for lobster, green, velvet and brown crab, Jonny hand-fishes for mackerel using darrows which have several hooks decorated with shiny foil to resemble small fish. Mackerel makes for great-tasting dishes on the menu. A widely undervalued fish, mackerel is plentiful in the summer months and a great alternative to tuna or other endangered fish species. I showcase this meaty fish in a lime-raw ceviche, or pan-seared in dill flour and served with horseradish mash and a trio of garden peas. Their opalescent blue and green tiger stripes and silvery body make them one of the most beautiful fish in the world. Mackerel must be eaten the day it is caught, otherwise most of the flavour and firmness is lost. A cheerful kitchen greeting is guaranteed upon his return if there is a pail of these shining beauties on Jonny's arm.

We try to buy line-caught fish and ethically farmed shellfish such as clams, mussels and oysters from local suppliers such as Inverlussa Mussels in Craignure, Ulva Oysters and Ardmore Fish in Salen. These bivalve molluscs must be grown in good quality water conditions to be safe for consumption, making them ecologically responsible choices. We are lucky to have crystal-clear waters and such high quality produce right on our doorstep.

Other Creatures in the Creels

Each lobster creel contains a mesh pouch in which bait is placed. Most fishermen here use frozen scad purchased from our local buying agent, but Jonny usually fishes for his own bait. He insists fresh bait attracts more crab and lobster.

Octopus, sea urchin, conger eel, red gurnard, spider crab and other virtually unsellable items are often hauled up in the creels as a by-catch. Making great dishes from all these wonderful underutilised treats is a part of my job I really enjoy.

Sea urchin roe (uni in Japan) is treasured at Ninth Wave. Its subtle and sexy, sea-fresh flavour is unveiled in many ways on our menu. It is best when eaten raw, enhanced with just-picked vegetables and a light touch. I also mix it in with Scallop Spring Roll filling, and as the prime ingredient in Sea Urchin and Red Onion Bisque with Ramsons and Dried Sea Urchin Croutons.

JONNY'S DAILY CRAB HAUL

Brown Crab (*Cancer pagurus*)

The meatiest of UK crabs, the brown is the most popular and versatile, and the one sold in most fishmongers in Scotland. It has good firm flesh that is ideal for everything from crab cakes, savoury cheesecake and salads, to seafood cocktails and sandwiches.

Spiny Spider Crab (*Maia squinado*)

This is less sweet and more robust-flavoured, with less white meat than other British crab. It has lots of loose, brown meat good for flavouring dishes such as risottos, bisques, Thai crab salads and spring rolls.

Velvet or Swimming Crab (*Necora puber*)

The velvet has the sweetest meat of all the British crabs. The best way to eat them is to take your time. Steam or boil up a bucketful, head for a spot in the sun with a friend, a lobster pick and a bottle of good wine. The brown meat is very bitter and not to be eaten raw. Whole velvets make lovely stock. The continentals eat them as a Sunday treat or on holidays.

Green Crab (*Carcinaes maenas*)

I have never seen these small beauties on a menu in Scotland, although thousands of tons are exported to Spain each year from Mull alone. The Italians like to eat them fried whole when their shells are soft, just after casting. They are marvellous for making crab stocks and soups.

Usually female crabs have more brown meat because of the more domed shape of their body. Males have more white meat because their claws are much bigger. You can tell their sex by looking at the purse or abdomen of the crab; the *males'* panel being narrow and the *females'* wider and rounded for egg carrying.

Landing Day

Landing day is the weekly event where all local boats bring their catches ashore for export. The crab and lobster, having been kept alive in storage cages in the sea, are brought by boat to the Fionnphort pier. In the early hours of Monday mornings the velvet and then green crabs are placed on huge, wooden steep-sided tables and sorted into large and medium sizes. They go into wooden slatted boxes that should weigh in at 9k net. Meanwhile the brown crab are placed into 30k stacking boxes, as are the lobsters before going off to the vivier lorry. Vivier lorries have huge aerated salt water tanks which keep the crustaceans alive for their journey to Spain.

Lively banter is often heard around the sorting table and is one of the highlights of Jonny's fishing week. It's the only time local fishermen get a chance to all get together to swap stories, pass on information and of course complain about the prices, the lack of lobsters and the weather. In the past a wee dram or two might be passed around after the sorting had been done. It was said this helped calm the winds and the fill the boats with luck. More likely it loosened their tongues and shortened the work day by quite a margin.

Another routine on landing day is to feed Nelson, the one-eyed seal. Nelson comes alongside the pier looking for any bits of fish that might be going spare. Although fishermen in general think of seals as thieves and nuisances (as they often steal bait from inside the creels) it is hard to resist Nelson's winsome charms.

Tourists are often enthralled at the sight of the all the rugged fishermen in their shiny suits of oilskin on the pier. And who can blame them? Unfortunately many visitors have the habit of thrusting their camera lenses into the faces of the local talent, which creates adverse reactions. I wonder how accountants, architects or anthropologists would feel if visitors to their area ran into their offices and started taking close-up photos of them without so much as a 'Would you mind if I take a photo?'

JONNY'S MOORING

When Jonny and I were first going out, I myself used to go on the boat with him. I was keen to show that Canadian girls can handle the great outdoors. That was before I got a creel rope wrapped around my leg and was almost dragged overboard. I have since lost my enthusiasm for throwing creels and voice my support from the relative comfort of the kitchen.

During a spell of fine, bright days Jonny was out lifting creels. One creel seemed to be so heavy it was making the hauler whine and struggle. When finally aboard, inside the lobster trap was a thrashing, mad mass of slick black coils. A six-foot conger eel can be a bit of a surprise even to a salty old seafarer like the husband. After the conger was neatly dispatched, when it was being filleted for use in the restaurant, a full-sized lobster was found in its stomach.

99

Apart from the excitement of the catch Jonny enjoys many aspects of being out on the water: the peace and solitude, the myriad of colours in the clear sea, and especially the dolphins when they frolic around the boat. In frosty weather, he loves the way the islands seem to stand up out of the water on their own reflections; a surreal perspective on the Treshnish Isles and Soay, all the islands in the boiling pot at the south of Iona. Jonny is the only fisherman in the area over 50 (he's 62) who single-handedly works a creel boat. Usually fishermen's bodies start to give them extreme grief when they are in their forties, so they hire younger guys to throw creels while they skipper the boat in the comfort of the wheelhouse.

The *Sonsie*, like all small boats hereabouts, fishes close into shore. Fleets of creels are dropped around the jagged, rocky outcrops that lobsters like to live in. John's boat is sturdy but slow, and his territory ranges from Ardalanish Point in the south to Camus to the north. All fishermen have their favourite spots and some are colourfully named: Tinker's Hole, the Black Stair and the Three Humps. The fishermen in our area are very careful to preserve stocks and use standard measuring tools to ensure that the regulations for minimum-sized lobsters are observed. This helps to protect the continuation both of the species and the fishing industry

Our friend and neighbour Jane the Diver lives in a house close by the Tor Mor Pier and John often sees her on his way home. Her house is perched on rocks right above the sea across from Eilean nam Ban, the island where the women of Iona (who were sent away in coracles by St Columba in 563) supposedly washed up. Jane's scallop boat can be seen pulled up on the pebbles in this sheltered cove. Jane, a tiny woman who is tough as nails, helps keep Ninth Wave supplied with hand-dived Mull scallops. They are the sweetest scallops ever. We've known Jane for decades and occasionally catch up over a cuppa (or a dram depending on the time) to chat about boat moorings, the weather and all things nautical. As well as being a first-class diver, Jane is also a qualified oceanographer, a stalwart supporter of the restaurant and a good laugh. She has even been known to waitress for us in an emergency.

LOBSTER FACTS

- A lobster takes an average of seven years to mature to keeping size in the UK.
- There are records from the 1800s of servants requesting not to have to eat lobsters more than three times a week.
- It is thought that lobsters can live up to 100 years old.
- The largest lobster on record was caught in Nova Scotia, Canada, and weighed 20.15kg (44lbs).
- Despite sporting more than 20,000 'eyes', lobsters have awful vision and communicate by smell and by sensing movement with their antennae.
- There is an albino lobster named Santa Claws who is believed to be about 30 years old and lives at the Weymouth Sea Life Centre.
- Lobsters with no claws are called pistols in the US.
- Lobsters have a brain the size of a grasshopper's.

Bog myrtle (also known as sweet gale) is sometimes picked by John on the way back from the boat. Bog myrtle, traditionally used to flavour beer or as a strewing herb, has a fresh, resiny scent not unlike eucalyptus or pine. We add a sprig to our Highland Fling cocktail which is made with a small batch of Scottish gin that has been infused with bog myrtle, heather and rowan during the distillation.

After a hard day of navigating, baiting and throwing creels, Jonny steam backs into the mooring. During most months the sun has already begun to set in its peachy glow behind the outline of Iona. It is then that he has time to band the lobsters and cut the crab. Both these procedures are carried out to ensure that the animals do not injure each other when stored in the underwater keep cages. All the tools and surfaces are then rinsed in the sea and set out ready for the next day's fishing. He rows back to shore with his lobster bucket in his dinghy, occasionally catching a glimpse of the cheerful otters that live in the cove.

SMOKED HADDOCK AND TOBERMORY TERROR CONSOMMÉ

This elegant soup is uniquely flavoured with an Isle of Mull Beer. It takes a while to make, but the divinely-tasting clear broth you end up with is well worth it.

Serves 4

1 tsp butter
380g/14oz carrots, sliced
180g/6½oz celery, chopped
140g/5oz white onion, chopped
100g/3½oz fennel bulb, chopped
30g/1oz shallots, sliced
1 tbsp coriander seeds
1 tsp cardamom
1 tsp turmeric
1 tsp cumin seeds
½ tsp fennel seeds
550ml/20fl oz Tobermory Terror
    Beer (or Guinness)
350ml/11fl oz water
1 tbsp dark soy sauce
5 fillets Mull smoked haddock
3 egg whites
40g/1½oz enoki or buna shimeji
    mushrooms
sprig tarragon
blanched julienne of carrot

Dry fry the spices in a medium-hot pan for two minutes, being careful to shake them lest they burn.

Place the butter in a large pot on medium low and add the carrots, celery, onions, shallots and fennel. Stir while gently cooking for 10 minutes, without colouring the vegetables.

Add the spices, beer, water and dark soy sauce and continue to simmer for 35 minutes.

Skin and debone four of the smoked haddock and save the best of the fillets for later. Add all the skin, bones and trimmings, plus one whole haddock fillet, to the vegetable mix in the pot. Simmer for 20 more minutes.

Strain the mixture and allow to cool. Refrigerate for an hour when cool. This will allow you to remove the solidified butter from off the top of the stock once it has chilled sufficiently.

When all the solid butter has been removed or strained off, place the stock in a large clean pot. Beat the three egg whites to the soft peak stage and add them to the pot of stock. Place the pot on high heat while whisking the egg whites constantly. Bring to the boil.

Turn down and simmer for 10 minutes. The liquid should now be clear and the egg white raft will have absorbed all the impurities.

Strain the soup through a muslin cloth and discard the whites. Season with sea salt to taste.

Bring a small pot of water to the boil and poach the four fillets in the water for two minutes. Drain.

Divide the clear consommé between the four serving bowls, placing a smoked haddock fillet in each bowl. Garnish with sautéed enoki mushrooms and thin strips of blanched carrots and a twist of black pepper.

WILD MULL SEA TROUT AND SHISO CEVICHE

Wild sea trout is such a rare treat we like to serve it this way to preserve its integrity. These Asian flavours also work well with salmon or freshwater trout.

Serves 2

230g/9oz sea trout fillets, skinned and boned
small handful of washed rocket
20g/¾oz diced mouli
1 small shallot, peeled and finely chopped
8 shiso leaves finely chopped (or a mix of mint and basil)
1 sprig dill chopped
zest of 1 kabosu (or lime)
2 kabosu (or limes) juiced
15g/½oz finely grated palm sugar
dry flaked sea lettuce
1 radish sliced
80ml/3fl oz of rapeseed oil
shiso and land cress to garnish

Dice the trout into 1cm cubes.

Place all the ingredients except for the trout and rocket into a non-metal bowl. Whisk well until the sugar is dissolved. Taste and add more salt and pepper if desired.

Add the trout and mix well into the marinade. Leave to rest for 10 minutes, covered, in the fridge. Mix in the mouli and drain off the excess marinade.

Serve in martini glasses or bowls on top of rocket leaves. Garnish with shiso, radish, landcress and kabosu wedges.

SEA URCHIN AND SCALLOP SPRING ROLLS

This recipe uses the sea-fresh roe that is found inside the sea urchins that Jonny sometimes catches in the creels. It is sold as uni in stores selling sushi foods. These crunchy rolls filled with garden vegetables are always popular.

Makes 8 rolls

3 tbsp vegetable oil
¼ tsp sesame oil
I carrot, julienned (cut into thin matchstick-sized strips)
I small red pepper, julienned
75g/2½oz Chinese cabbage, thinly sliced
½ small courgette, julienned
I celery stick, julienned
2 tbsp soy sauce
2 scallions, sliced thinly
I tbsp fresh ginger, peeled and grated
I clove garlic, minced
4 large sheets filo pastry, covered in plastic or loosely covered with a damp paper towel to prevent drying
4 large scallops, seared and sliced
8 pieces sea urchin roe (from 2 large sea urchins), chopped in half
I egg, beaten
cornflour for dusting
vegetable oil for frying

DIPPING SAUCE
75ml/2fl oz soy sauce
75ml/2fl oz black rice vinegar
I tsp honey
I tsp oyster sauce
I dash sesame oil
I small chilli sliced thinly

If using fresh sea urchin . . . hold the urchin upside-down with a very thick towel and, using a pair of small pointed scissors, break an opening through the mouth (the round nodule in the middle of its underside) and quickly snip the shell all the way around, leaving a round hole. Carefully remove the cut out cap and discard. Tip out the seawater. The edible parts are orange in colour and adhere to the shell in bands. Carefully scoop out the orange tongues of sea urchin meat with a small spoon. Rinse the pieces in a bowl of cold water. Set aside to drain on paper towel

Make the dipping sauce by whisking up all the ingredients. This can be made several days ahead and kept covered in the fridge.

Heat the oils in either a wok or a deep frying pan. Stir-fry the carrot, pepper, cabbage, courgette and celery for 3–4 minutes. Add the garlic and ginger and cook for 30 seconds while stirring. Then put into the pan the sea urchin roe, scallop pieces, water chestnuts, spring onions and soy sauce and stir thoroughly. Turn off the heat after a minute when the liquid has disappeared. Allow the mixture to cool.

Cut the filo sheets lengthways in half to give 8 long strips. Make only one roll at a time, leaving the other pastry well covered to prevent it drying out and becoming unusable. Spoon an 1/8th of the mixture into a sausage shape and place near one short end of the filo.

Brush the edges of the filo with beaten egg. Fold the shorter sides of the wrapper in (the sides that run at right angles to the mixture). Roll the filling forward tightly until all the pastry is rolled over the filling and you end up with a cylinder that is sealed at both ends.

Place the rolls on a surface or plate lightly dusted with cornflour and cover them with a damp (not wet) towel while you finish rolling all of them.

Heat 3.5cm of oil in a deep pan to 375C. Fry the rolls a few at a time, until the skins are crisp and golden brown, turning them as they brown. Drain the rolls on kitchen towels to get rid of excess oil and serve them at once for best results. To do the Ninth Wave presentation, cut the ends off square, slice each roll diagonally and stand them on end.

GARDEN COURGETTE BLOSSOMS STUFFED WITH LANGOUSTINES

The taste of these summer favourites is a harmonious blend of garden and sea. I have also made them with cooked octopus, lobster, crab or a combination of these. We serve them with a herb hollandaise, but Jonny likes his with caper tartar sauce and a pint of homebrew. They are a bit fiddly to make, but so moreish.

Serves 6

6 blossoming baby courgettes
nasturtium flowers and leaves for
　garnish
sea salt

FILLING
240g/8½oz cooked langoustines
60g/2oz cream cheese
1 small egg
1 tsp plain flour
½ tsp lemon, fine zest
30g/1oz smoked Mull cheddar
½ tsp chives
½ tsp ransoms (wild garlic)
1 tsp nasturtium leaves
dash Worcester sauce
sea salt
black pepper

TEMPURA BATTER
150ml/5fl oz ice-cold Isle of Mull
　Galleon Gold Beer (or soda
　water)
1 egg
dash Worcester sauce
dash fish sauce

In a food processor, mix the cream cheese, egg, flour, lemon zest, cheese, Worcester sauce, a pinch of salt and a twist of pepper, for five seconds or so. Chop up the cooked langoustines and place in a processor. Mix for five seconds. Place the mixture into a medium-sized bowl. Add the finely chopped chives, ramsons and nasturtium leaves and mix with a wooden spoon. Season with additional salt and pepper to taste.

Hold the baby courgette and flower by the courgette end. Be careful when handling not to snap the flowers off the courgettes. If the blossom is closed, use your thumbs to gently make a split in the flower. With your fingertips, snap off the yellow stamens in the centre of the flower and discard. Trim off any green hairy spikes at the base of the flower where it meets the courgette. Repeat with the remaining flowers. Shake to remove any insects or dirt that may be on the flower. Rinse the courgette under cold water, being careful not to get the flower wet. Dry the courgette.

Fill a piping bag with a plain 1cm diameter hole in the end (or a medium round tip) with the langoustine mix. Pipe into the courgettes, dividing the mixture amongst the flowers. I cannot tell you how much to put in each one, as the flowers can be different sizes. You want enough for a decent taste but not so much that it oozes out of the flower. Gently pinch the flowers shut around the filling.

On a cutting board, using a sharp paring knife and starting at free end of the courgette, slice it almost in half, to three-quarters down its length, forming two prongs. Be careful not to cut all the way to the flower, as it will fall apart.

For the batter, place the egg, fish sauce, Worcester sauce and beer in a bowl and whisk well. Then add the flours and whisk slowly until only just mixed. Do not over-mix – lumps are ok.

Line a tray with kitchen paper. Fill a deep saucepan or deep-fryer one-third full with oil, then heat over medium heat to 180C. Working in batches of four, dip the courgettes one at a time into the batter, allowing the excess to drain off, then deep-fry for two minutes or until golden. Using a metal slotted spoon, transfer to a tray. Repeat with the remaining flowers and batter.

Sprinkle immediately with sea salt. Place on a plate with nasturtium garnishes and serve hot.

 THE CROFT

croft (kroft) noun: A small farm in Scotland comprising a plot of arable land attached to a house, with a share in the common grazing land for pasturing livestock.

All year round on the croft you can tell what month it is just by looking at the colourful swathe that is our lower field. The wildflowers, the reeds, the washes of spring green to mauves to gold, russet and beyond are ever-changing, a crofter's calendar in 3D. On rare occasions, before my long cooking day begins, I stand just outside the restaurant door in the mornings, tea in hand, with my eyes closed, to breathe in the evocative perfume of the landscape. I can now tell the subtle differences in the redolent air: the sweetness of meadowsweet, the tropical smell of whin blossoms or the faint, rusty, spiciness of brambles long fallen.

Bruach Mhor, meaning big green bank in Gaelic, has been used for agriculture for hundreds of years. Generations of families worked this land and other crofts in the immediate area, which were set up by the Duke of Argyll in the late 1700s for fishing crofters. Back then there were thirty fishermen living in Bunessan and Fionnphort (then named Caol-Ithe, meaning the sound of Iona). John and his parents bought the croft and Bruach Mhor House in 1981. John convinced his parents that self-sufficiency was the way to go and they sold their house on the east coast in North Queensferry and moved onto the croft with John, his first wife, and their two kids. After five years of battling the Hebridean winters and all that rural life here entails, they sold the big house to our present neighbour Derek and his partner Heather, and moved back to the east coast. The farmland and bothy was gifted to John by his parents.

The Croft is a wild and largely edible landscape. Over 70 edible herbs, greens and edible flowers abound here. During the last twenty years, most of our acreage has been allowed to revert to its natural state. Since the croft has been sheep-free, the native plants and animals have not only returned, but have flourished on this sunny southern peninsula of Mull. We try to make use of as much of the croft's many wild foods and flowers as possible. I build our menus around tasty foraged ingredients such as berries, mushrooms, sorrel, angelica, bog myrtle and pignuts, to name a few.

Flower cookery, which can be traced back to Roman times, features prominently at Ninth Wave. Since we've opened, I have been endeavouring genuinely to understand the taste and textures of these foraged ingredients and not just use them to jump on the trend bandwagon. As an integral part of our dishes, I feel they should stand out. I use foraged flowers raw in salads and on sashimi, cooked in sauces, powdered, and crystallised. Flowers can be unique seasoning tools. Some flowers are very peppery, such as nasturtiums from which we make flower tempura and seafood butter, dried hogweed seeds and carnation petals with their undertones of cardamom and clove respectively, which are great accompaniments to both our Wild Mull Venison and Treshnish Lamb. The flavour of certain blooms can also be wonderfully refreshing palate cleansers. At the restaurant I make a sorbet from borage flowers with their subtle cucumber flavour along with sorrel and its acidic lemon tang, with green apple.

Other edible blossoms on the Ninth Wave croft include pansies, primrose, mallow, angelica, dandelion, burnet, hyssop, snapdragons, clover, chickweed, lavender, rosa rugosa, thyme, meadowsweet, mugwort and marigold. When foraging for flowers I am always delighted to come across tiny shimmering lizards, toads and golden-patterned slow-worms (which are kind enough to eat the slugs), and occasionally a magical, snuffling hedgehog. Blooms of the elderflower, bramble and clover that abound here attract bumblebees, honey bees, hoverflies and drone flies which help pollinate our isle.

Across from the restaurant there thrives a black elderflower tree we call 'The Ogre'. Fifteen years ago I bought a 6-inch high Black Beauty seedling from a plant nursery and brought it home. It warned on the label that it 'needs lots of space to spread and can reach up to 8 feet in height'. Because of the extreme winds and salt in Fionnphort, most trees and shrubs end up as stunted versions of themselves. So I planted the delicate-looking, purply-black sapling only three feet from the caravan and hoped for the best. The Ogre is now home to a family of blackbirds, and is 12 feet tall and 7 feet wide despite rather vicious pruning sessions. We do not begrudge him his place, however, as we pick the pink, slightly lemony blossoms to make into a crisp sparkling rosé wine, which I then use in several of our desserts such as Rhubarb and Black Elderflower Wine Quiver (a layered, intensely flavoured jelly).

A very special ingredient can be found in the fields around Bruach Mhor from June to October. Jonny, the Old Sea Dog, and Steve, our Hungarian handyman, can often be found with a trowel in hand, digging nuts from under certain white-flowered umbelliferae, in search of the much coveted pignut, hognut or arnut (*Conopodium majus*). Locally known as lady nuts, this underground tuber or corm is small and brown like a hazelnut, and its sweet, aromatic flavour has been compared to that of the chestnut. I think it tastes like a slightly nutty sweet turnip when eaten raw. It is very nutritious and staves off hunger, which was probably one of the reasons it was so popular. If you collected enough nuts they could be dried and ground into flour to make bread. Several of the old folks in Fionnphort have told me they remember hunting for these savoury treats in the fields while walking to and from Creich School.

During the season we are able to gather whin (gorse) blossoms for ice cream and panna cotta and syrup. Their proliferation of neon-yellow blooms

WHIN

gorse, furze (Gaelic *conasg* meaning prickly)
Genus *Ulex*
Spiny shrub and a member of the pea family

O yellow Whin in the wood!
O yellow Broom in the pines!
Your goldenness is wondrous good,
And with your scent combines
To image delicate wines.
O eyes of the life of the world!
O breaths of the world's perfume!
Small sprites lie close within you curled,
And twinkle through the Broom,
And the Whin's light illume.

James Carnegie (Earl of Southesk) 1877.

Whin abounds on the Ross of Mull. It is nutritious and is a wild fodder for cattle and sheep in the area. A generation ago it was still cut, dried and crushed for winter feed here. You can see its cheery blossoms anytime from January to November depending on the weather and the species. I often see linnets, stonechats and finches feeding amongst its thorns.

IN THE PAST . . .

- In parts of Scotland the flowers were also used to flavour and add colour to whisky, wine and tea.

- Strewn chopped-up whin branches were used here to keep birds and rodents off newly planted food crops.

- In the Highlands whin was sacred to Cailleach Bheur (the blue hag) bringer of winter, who also protected animals during this season.

- The barbed nature of the plant means that it was thought to have protective capabilities and purportedly kept witches at bay.

- In the 1800s Scottish bakers often used this intensely hot-burning wood to heat their ovens.

- For rich Scots in the past, flower buds were collected and pickled with blades of mace and peppercorns, in a white wine vinegar and salt solution can be seen all around Fionnphort for a good part of the year. We love to see the whin's vivid gold flowers, as it is often the only spot of summer colour to be seen during the dour and dreich winter months that follow. You can smell their strong, coconutty fragrance wafting across the croft, especially when they are warmed by the sun. To pick them, I wear two pairs of garden gloves, as whins have deadly sharp one-inch spikes all around the flowers. Chain mail would be better. When picking these in a gale force 8 wind it is wise to use a bucket with a lid on it, as most of my harvest was blown away to Iona the first time I tried it. I was left bereft, in my tatty oilskin dungarees, with an empty fishing bucket, feeling like a human pin-cushion after all the thorns. Sorry to ruin your image of me frolicking through sunshiny fields with a painted wooden trug, in flowing diaphanous skirts of floral design.

The meadowsweet season arrives in mid-July. It is in this wonderfully sun-filled month that I start gathering the fragrant, feathery fronds for making some of our signature dishes. I am completely sold on this heady, decadent-smelling wonder, with its dramatic froth of graceful white flowers. It also attracts bees and other wildlife, making it an important part of a healthy ecosystem. At tea break during this time of year, Steve and Fédra, our lovely Hungarians (who have lived on the croft and worked with us for three years), and I love to watch the fields of meadowsweet sway in the breeze while we chat about goings on.

The Lady of the Meadow has inspired me to create aromatic panna cotta, almond nougat, and rich ice cream. Our meadowsweet cordial is vital to flavour ganache for sinfully good white chocolate truffles or to pour onto my morning porridge. A little goes a long way – meadowsweet is no shrinking violet. The florets can be dried for a more subtle enhancement to sprinkle over desserts or flavour yoghurts and crumble toppings. An often unnoticed part of this plant, the dark green leaves, add a lovely mellow taste to salads, ices and fruit punch. You can freeze the blooms for winter use, but make sure they are double bagged and in an airtight container, because the smell and taste can permeate everything else in the freezer. Meadowsweet wasn't used as an ancient strewing herb and air-freshener for nothing. In the Hebrides meduart (as the plant is called in certain regions of Scotland) was also used long ago to treat headache and fever.

In medieval times, meadowsweet blossom was used to flavour mead, the honeyed tipple of the druids. Analysis of Bronze Age pollen grains has also shown that people in the Orkney Isles also used meadowsweet as a floral tribute at burial sites.

CROFT MEADOWSWEET CORDIAL

Wonderful in cocktails, on yoghurt and over pancakes.

1 litre/1¾ pt water
1kg/2¼lb vanilla caster sugar
12 large meadowsweet flower
    heads
5 fronds of sweet cicely or a ¼
    tsp chervil seeds or a pinch of
    ground star anise
zest and juice of 1 lemon and 1
    pink grapefruit (unwaxed and
    washed)

Shake the meadowsweet to remove any insects. Pour the water and sugar into a saucepan. Grate in the zest of the fruit and heat, stirring as it comes to a boil and the sugar dissolves. Pour the hot syrup over the meadowsweet and sweet cicely and leave covered overnight in the fridge. Next day bring the syrup to the boil. Remove from the heat and strain. Juice the fruits and add to the syrup.

Pour into clean sterile bottles and fill with syrup. Cap with corks or metal bottle caps. Refrigerate after opening.

When we can steal a few minutes off from the kitchen in the autumn, and it's not raining, we use the time to collect brambles. It is not the romantic idyll of casually snatching mouthfuls of glistening berries with a troop of laughing children trailing behind, dancing in beams of glorious sun. It is often very windy, the thigh-high reeds very wet, and wellies and a waxed jacket are necessities. The best berries are always in the middle of the drainage ditch, which means forging into it up to your armpits while trying not to get shredded to pieces. On the other side of the barbed-wire fence of our neighbours, Mary and Gerry, the blackberries seem grow into bigger, more luscious orbs that hang in profusion, just begging to be placed on the tongue in reverence. So, when not wading into water-filled ditches, I spend most of my brambling time on my knees, reaching though the fence. If the barbed-wire doesn't get you, the thistles will. If the thistles don't get you, the nettles will. If the nettles don't get you, the berry thorns definitely will! I often come back with my pail of berries looking like a dishevelled bag lady who has been mud-wrestling with a sabre-tooth tiger.

Once I was so intent on reaching as many brambles as I could that I got both my coat sleeves and my waist-long hair inextricably tangled in the barbed wire. Every movement made it worse, and I ended up with each arm pinned fast, somewhat like a gassed moth specimen in a glass cabinet. I had visions of being trapped there until Dave the Post discovered me when he delivered the mail at 4 o'clock. But when I heard the predatory shriek of a giant buzzard getting closer and closer, somehow I found the strength to break free. The next day I noticed that I had left behind a tuft of hair (which matched a curious bald spot on the left side of my head) and a scrap of material from my jacket.

This year I got Stevie Wonder, our famous Hungarian tractor repairman, builder, locksmith, goulash-maker and handyman, to do the dirty work and as a result got a record-breaking 18kg of brambles from the aforementioned ditch. After presenting our diners with Fresh Bramble, Black Jelly, Whin Blossom Cream and Dark Valrhona Chocolate Millefeuille and other delights, the remaining crop is made into our unique chutney. Our Bramble, Beetroot and Ras-el-Hanout Chutney is a zingy and popular component of our all-Scottish cheeseboard.

I really do love living and working at Bruach Mhor. Despite harping on about the pitfalls and tribulations of life on Mull, I can't think of a place I'd rather be. How many chefs get to walk from the kitchen straight out into

SPICY BRAMBLE AND BEETROOT CHUTNEY (SEE P. 125)

the countryside, to enjoy the fresh air with red admirals quivering, kestrels soaring and drunken bees bumbling all around them? And in the wild winter, when the restaurant is closed and the elements relentlessly batter our wee bothy, I find comfort in my store of perfect rows of gem-hued jars: jams, jellies, vinegars, chutneys, syrups and infused oils. They speak to me of the kinder seasons, a portent of all the wonderful harvests that are to come.

When we had free time, before Ninth Wave, Jonny and I used to cut peats on the croft for the bothy fire. The smell of peat is incredibly evocative, romantic even. It conjures up images of heath land, an old tobacconist's shop, wet tweed and hot toddies. The peat-cutting tool is a half-moon shaped blade of metal on a long pole, like a lawn-edger but much bigger. I wielded it with typically Canadian enthusiasm. John and I surprisingly still have all our toes, but he could never use those particular wellies again.

Foraged ingredients such as wild flowers will continue to feature on Ninth Wave's menu, and with an errant eye, I am keenly watching the multitude of ways in which they are helping to re-establish the identity of British cuisine across the board.

MEADOWSWEET AND HEATHER HONEY ICE CREAM

I pair the nectar-like taste of the meadowsweet with Scottish heather honey and a hint of Madagascan vanilla. For quality control purposes I feel honour-bound to sample several dollops of this lip-smacking concoction before it makes it to the freezer.

Serves 4

350ml/12fl oz double cream
180ml/6fl oz milk
30ml/1fl oz heather honey
30g/1oz caster sugar
30g/1oz meadowsweet flowers
    stemmed
½ pod vanilla seeds,
10 medium egg yolks, beaten
pinch of sea salt

On the lowest heat, cook the first six ingredients in a heavy-bottomed pot for 20 minutes.

Stir occasionally and do not boil.

Place the beaten egg yolks in a large bowl. Strain the meadowsweet cream mix into the egg yolks while whisking vigorously. Place the mixture into a clean pot and cook on a low heat while stirring constantly with a wooden spoon, making sure to thoroughly scrape the bottom and corners of the pot. The mix will thicken and begin to steam. Over-cooking at this point scrambles the eggs, so be careful.

The custard is ready when you can draw a clear line through it on the back of the wooden spoon. Cover and cool in the fridge. Finish in an ice-cream maker as per manufacturer's instructions.★

★If you don't have an ice-cream maker, put the mix in a plastic Tupperware container and put in the freezer, stirring well every 15 minutes until solid, to break up the ice crystals.

MEADOWSWEET AND HEATHER HONEY ICE CREAM AND
BRAMBLE AND BLACK ELDERFLOWER SORBET

121

BRAMBLE AND BLACK ELDERFLOWER SORBET

The amount of glucose syrup needed here varies depending on the sweetness of the brambles. Over-sweeten slightly to taste, as sorbets lose some of their sweetness when frozen.

Serves 4

425g/1lb brambles
230ml/7fl oz water
115ml/3½fl oz black elderflower wine **or**
15g/½oz of dried elderberry powder soaked in 115ml/3½fl oz rosé wine
30g/1oz caster sugar
110ml/3½fl oz glucose syrup (or to taste)
30ml/1fl oz lemon juice
2 drops real essential mandarin oil

Put all the ingredients into a medium sized pot and stir over a high heat and bring to the boil. Cover and simmer on low for 5 minutes. Puree in a food processor or with a hand blender. Push through a sieve and cool.

Finish in an ice-cream maker as per manufacturer's instructions. (If you don't have an ice-cream maker, see note on p. 120.)

RED CURRANT AND CHOCOLATE PORT GRANITA

Certain 'Ladies Who Lunch' in Fionnphort have a penchant for Rubis liqueur, and this lush summer treat pays homage to them all.

Serves 4

400g/14oz red currants
140g/5oz caster sugar
1 lemon, zest and juice
100ml/3fl oz Rubis chocolate liqueur (or port)
70ml/2½fl oz water
pinch of sea salt

Put all the ingredients into a large pan and cook gently until the currants have burst. Whizz with a hand blender, then push through a sieve.

Pour into a small shallow tray or casserole and freeze for at least two hours until solid. Let it rest five minutes at room temperature before serving. Scrape with the tines of a fork to end up with fine granules. Serve in small glasses.

RED CURRANT AND CHOCOLATE PORT GRANITA

WHITE CHOCOLATE AND WILD FLOWER GANACHE

You can make this in just over an hour, but if you leave the ganache to set overnight it is much easier to dip.

Makes 80–90 pieces

130g/4½oz cream
120ml/4fl oz whin blossoms (or
   25g/1oz other, such as rose,
   elderflower or lemon geranium)
680g white chocolate callets (chips)
1 tbsp soft butter
tempered white chocolate
   couverture for dipping

Making the ganache

Place the chocolate in a large bowl. Bring the cream to the boil and pour over the chocolate and stir until smooth. Cool for five minutes, then mix in the softened butter.

Line a 30cm by 30cm by 2cm baking tray smoothly with clingfilm. The size does not have to be exact; the bigger the pan, the shallower and wider your chocolates will be.

123

Pour the ganache into the lined pan and allow it to cool to room temperature; once it has cooled to room temperature, cover with cling film and place in a cool room for 24 hours to set.

Using a straight (not serrated) hot knife, cut into the desired shapes – rectangles, squares or triangles. When the squares have come to room temperature, drop into the tempered chocolate and lift out using a fork or dipping tool.

Allow the excess chocolate to run off, then scrape the fork against the rim of your bowl to remove any remaining excess.

Place onto a tray lined with greaseproof paper, working from top to bottom and right to left. Before the chocolate solidifies you can add decorations, such as candied petals, sea salt or grated chocolate. Store in an airtight container in a cool room for up to two weeks.

SPICY CROFT BRAMBLE AND BEETROOT CHUTNEY

A great way to turn a glut of berries into a year-long treat. Use fresh picked berries immediately after picking, as the pectin levels, responsible for thickening the chutney, deteriorate quickly. This exotic spicy chutney features on our cheeseboard and is especially memorable with the Isle of Mull Cheddar.

2 kg/4½lb blackberries
640g/1lb 6oz red onions, sliced
540g/1lb cooked beetroot, diced
4 cloves garlic, pureed
2 red chilli, minced
540g/1lb dark brown sugar
600ml/1 pt cider vinegar
4 tbsp fresh ginger, grated
4 tsp ras-el-hanout

Wash the brambles. Drain well.

On medium, heat the oil in a large pot on the stove top. Add the onions, chillies and fry for four minutes on a low-medium heat until softened. Add the garlic and ginger and cook for one more minute, stirring constantly.

Add remaining ingredients except for the beetroot. Turn the heat up to high and bring to the boil. Strain the berries etc, saving the liquid. Put a third of the liquid back into the pot with the strained berries. Simmer on a low-medium heat uncovered for 15–20 minutes. Put the rest of the strained liquid in a medium-sized pot and bring to the boil. Lower the heat slightly and boil until reduced to half the volume. Add the beetroot and the reduction to the simmered berries.

Spoon into warm sterilised jars. Cover and seal immediately. Store in a cool, dark and dry place until required.

 AN ISLAND GARDEN

While from a wildlife or ecological perspective our natural croft is a haven, from a gardening standpoint it is an absolute nightmare. It is a constant, no-holds-barred fight, raged against a multitude of creatures and seven acres of weeds: ground elder, sorrel, yarrow, buttercup, nettles, dockens, reeds, couch grass, rosebay willowherb . . .

In Fionnphort we have all the normal pests that annoy gardeners everywhere in Britain: cutworms, slugs, aphids, carrot-fly, bean-weevil, and rhubarb-boring beetle. As an added bonus we also have to guard against salt-laden gales, rabbits, voles, mice, birds, cattle, sheep and, of course, red deer. Armed with eight-foot deer fencing above ground, two feet of rabbit mesh dug underground, live traps, garlic spray, hedges, miles of fruit netting and mint imperials to keep our spirits up, we usually manage to fend off most attacks. Despite all these adversities we really love putting time and effort into the garden. Our whole menu is based on the freshest of the fresh. It's quite astounding that anyone gardens here, but garden they do. Ninth Wave is glad to be part of the 36-member strong Ross of Mull and Iona Organic Gardening Association.

Across the parking lot from the restaurant lies our veg garden. Our plot is about 600 square yards and hosts a small greenhouse used for fair-weather produce such as shiso and basil, tomatoes, chillies, aubergines and squash. I love using shiso herb (also known as perils) a member of the mint family which is used a lot in Japanese cooking. Another new favourite is my kaffir lime tree which also lives in the greenhouse. Its unique perfumey, citrus profile goes wonderfully well with both shellfish and poultry.

At the end of the season the greenhouse must be dismantled to save it from being reduced to shards in the winter storms, but some plants can over-winter in our orangery. Steve and Jonny built the grand-sounding orangery out of recycled house windows and some breeze blocks last February.

Our veg garden and greenhouses are not picture-perfect, but functional and rustic. To keep the weeds down we use old tin sheets (under which the common lizards and slowworms like to live) held down with used tires. Along with our huge compost bins, piles of seaweed fertilizer, rainwater butts and homemade poly tunnels it is hardly attractive, but the taste, oh, the taste of that veg!

This garden provides the restaurant with all its lovely greens, carrots, beans, peas, beetroot, spinach, kale, rhubarb, cabbage, chard and tatties for

the season. We find it fascinating to grow old-fashioned herbs and vegetables such as purslane, comfrey, buckwheat, sunflowers, salad burnet, burdock and salsify to revive traditional locally foraged and grown foods. We make our garden a bit bigger every year to help keep the restaurant supplied with more fresh produce. This year we may have been overly optimistic and have started a caged fruit garden, complete with cherries, plums, striped tiger figs, honeyberries and damsons, which keep our lone blush apple tree company. The trees are surrounded by a host of berries. Every time I come home with the unheard-of wonders of Japanese wineberries, grapes or strawberry spinach Jonny rolls his eyes and cries, 'And chust where da ye think we're going to put these?'

A Scotsman and his Tatties

Although I'd worked in restaurant kitchens for 14 years when I arrived in Scotland, I wasn't prepared for the 'Great Tattie Debate'. As a city girl I stupidly announced to a bar full of locals at the Keel Row pub, 'A potato's a potato'. Little did I know you could be stoned to death with sheep turnips if you uttered such blasphemy around here. Dismayed and more than a little disgusted at my lack of knowledge in the tuber department, Jonny set out to educate me.

'Weel now [pause for dramatic island effect], there's yer waxy salads, yer starchy mashers, yer fluffy roasters, the all-roonders and yer in-betwixt,' he said with a unfamiliar steely look in his usually far-away fisherman's eyes (some fishermen and sailors have a habit of looking into a far corner of the room while talking, developed from long hours at sea scanning the horizon).

Tatties are a very serious subject on Mull indeed. My dear husband must consume his weekly quota of 10lbs of potatoes or he gets rather cranky and starts to show signs of bag-lady syndrome.

Throughout spring, summer and autumn Jonny can often be seen lifting tatties for the restaurant, gamely followed by his buddy 'Bolshy Mungo', the robin. Mungo waits for him to unearth rotund worms and then flick

130

them over to him on the tines of the garden fork. Every time Jonny turns to wash off the tatties, Mungo perches right on the fork handle to get his own worms.

John used to work as an organic gardener at Carsaig Estate, near Pennyghael and nearby Ardfenaig. His passion to grow fruit and veg is equal to his love of the sea, and as he often finds there are not enough hours in a Mull day for both, his favourite expression is 'Christ, is that the time already?' Undoubtedly, Jonny's favourite part of his garden is the tattie patch. Row after row of neat triangular mounds of dark earth, so shaped for easy digging and effective watering.

JONNY'S TOP TATTIES FOR A MULL GARDEN

First Earlies

Duke of York. Tastes like a potato should. Good nutty, waxy all-rounder big enough to store for winter.

Anya (a cross between Desiree and Pink Fir Apple). Nubbly, yellow, sweet salad potato that holds its shape well when cooked.

Second Earlies

Charlotte. Creamy, mild salader, just scrub and boil.

Nicola. Similar taste to Charlotte but with better blight resistance.

Maris Peer. Fast finishing. Produces lots of cream-coloured medium to large potatoes.

Early Mains

Lady Balfour. Reliable spud. Excellent all-rounder, disease resistant, flavoursome.

Maris Piper. Good, tasty multi-purpose potato, especially good for chips.

Late Mains

Valor. Slightly sweet and buttery, good for mashing, boiling or chipping.

Pink Fir Apple. The King of salad potatoes. Extraordinary flavour, creamy and delicious. Elongated, bumpy appearance and hard to clean, though.

TRIVIA

In our house there is a clear preference for waxy potatoes such as Pink Fir Apple and Lady Balfour, that don't explode into shrapnel when you boil them like Kerr's Pink or Golden Wonder. Although he tries at least one new potato variety a year (out of curiosity), we grow four major crops of potato for the kitchen each year. First Earlies, Second Earlies, Early Maincrop, and Late Maincrop.

The extremely wet weather on Mull makes choosing the correct varieties important. As I sit and write this in early September we have had three straight weeks of torrential rain and many days of gale force 6 to 9 winds. All the usual claims for blight-resistant and pest-defiant strains of seed potatoes mean nothing here. I think the plant descriptions must be written by tiny, bespectacled gardeners living in tamest Shropshire, not strapping, tartan-clad Hielanders howkin' spadefuls in the midgy wilderness of a Hebridean Isle.

Tatties were being grown in Scotland as early as 1598. Blight (a fungus which resides in the ground) has persisted on the island since the potato famine which ravaged the population of Mull and Iona from 1846 to 1857. Rotating the crop location helps, but even when our potatoes remain blight-free, the battle against black leg, soft rot and slug damage is still to be won. It's quite amazing we manage to grow 100% of Ninth Wave's potatoes, given the odds against it here.

Without being fanatical or thrusting the eco banner in everyone's face, we are founded on green ethics. The restaurant and adjoining house was renovated sympathetically, using as much recycled material as possible. We collect rain water for garden watering, use organic methods and natural wildlife deterrents. We don't go in much for eco-lingo, but practise what seems to us to be common sense though Jonny insists it is 'nae so common'. Jonny has several tricks up his gardening boiler suit sleeve, such as planting a cut piece of rhubarb near each brassica's root to ward off club root and using wood ash from the fire to enrich the legume trenches. Every winter we gather truckloads of seaweed that has been washed ashore during storms, to put on the garden for fertilizer. Most of it breaks down or is turned into soil except for the wiry varieties that seem to be as biodegradable as plastic. We also plant mustard as green mulch which gets rotovated under to improve the nutrients in the soil.

During the summer I pick the flowering baby courgettes myself. At 6 pm at the beginning of service set-up I go out to the garden to gather flowers and herbs for plating. Because we have so much fresh crab coming off the boat every day I love to use it in our *Tempura Baby Courgettes with Herby Hollandaise and Whole Crab Claw*. The first night we had it on the menu we sold out very quickly, as only five courgettes were ready for picking. The male blooms grow on thin stems, whereas the females are attached to the end of the small courgettes. The Italians are crazy about stuffed zucchini flowers too, and they seem to be re-appearing on many U.K. restaurant menus.

Another treat from our garden is the prolific but rarely seen land cress. Rocket and spicy greens are very popular these days. Land or American cress tastes like a very intense and peppery watercress. The leaves are a bit tougher in texture than watercress or rocket. It is easy to grow and keeps on going pretty much all year long if the frost stays away. I love mixing it with sweeter greens such as butter lettuce and Little Gem.

Pickling no longer has to involve 100 Mason jars, a glut of veg and ye olde box of pickling spice. Restaurants these days pickle baby veg and fruit only hours before service. Baby turnips, carrots, beetroot, green beans, and exotic mushrooms are just a few of the things going under the brine lately. There has been a resurgence in old-fashioned methods of preserving and in experimenting with fresher and faster versions of old standbys. If it's a vegetable which is good eaten raw, you can use them just washed. If not, you can blanch them in boiling water, steam them lightly, or roast them before brining. You want them with a bit of crunch left in them.

GARDEN PRODUCE AND PICKLING BRINE

500g/1lb just picked vegetables or
    fruit
240ml/8fl oz vinegar
240ml/8fl oz water
Flavouring/spices (see below)
115g/4oz sugar
15g/½oz sea salt or kosher salt

Method: toss raw or blanched vegetables with half the salt in a bowl and let stand for 30 minutes. Drain in a sieve but do not rinse.

Heat the vinegar, flavouring/spices, sugar and remaining salt in a small saucepan over a medium-low heat, stirring until the sugar has dissolved. Remove from the heat and add the vegetables. Transfer to a plastic bowl and marinate, chilled, at least 2 hours. Store in an airtight container until use.

Make your own pickling combinations:

For vinegars try: white or red wine vinegar, cider, raspberry, tarragon, sherry, malt, beer, coconut or rice.

For sugars try: caster, muscovado, maple, Demerara, palm, agave syrup or honey.

For flavouring add: fresh herbs, fennel or cumin seeds, red pepper flakes, mustard seed, Sichuan peppercorns, hibiscus flowers, geranium leaves, juniper, allspice berries, coriander seeds, fenugreek, cloves of garlic, jalapeños, harissa, rose petals, capers or citrus zest.

Always store in a sterilized air-tight container. Refrigerator pickles will keep for about a month. We use pickled Sichuan cucumbers with our smoked mackerel, pickled chervil mouli with salmon, pickled rice wine ginger with our venison carpaccio, and pickled brambles with pâtés.

We use stacks of old fishing creels as windbreaks for the sheds and gardens. While on the way to dig the pea trench one sunny day in July, Jonny heard an odd snuffling noise which seemed to be coming from the large willows by the garden. That sound didn't belong to a tree-dweller, that was for sure. Then he saw something move in one of the higher rows in the pile of creels. He went to investigate and found the creature. A tiny male hedgehog was caught in one of the crab traps. He had crawled in the open eye of the creel and couldn't find his way out. The creels are usually left with the doors open just in case birds or animals venture in, but somehow this one had blown shut. Hedgehogs are wonderful. Not only are they adorable-looking, but they eat all the garden pests like slugs, snails, grasshoppers and caterpillars. Jonny brought the furze-pig into the kitchen for us to see before letting him loose on the croft.

Last spring I had Steve build me a raised herb-bed out of pink granite. It is just by the door near the kitchen so I can pop outside just before service and gather my herbs and flowers. My approach to choosing what to put in my herb bed is to go by name and rarity. It's been almost a year since I planted a shipment of live plants that I ordered from the Apple and Tree Man Nursery in Perth. I ordered culinary plants that are no longer used much. I'd never even heard of most of them, quite frankly. I've always been a word lover, so some of them just stuck out, so strange were their names: orpine (which to me, sounds like a swooning Shakespearean maid) and hottentot fig (which could have been a 1920s dance) were the best of the selection. A bit more pre-purchase research would have been handy. I ended up with some inappropriate and downright absurd things just because of their names.

The purple plantain and sweet cicely specimens sadly expired within two days of planting. The husband was very supportive during this traumatic time, supplying copious amounts of tissues, cups of soothing tea and a large plastic tuba for comic relief.

CARLA'S WEIRD HERB LOTTERY

The Hopefuls

Orpine (also called Live Forever) is my new favourite because of its name, cheerfully fleshy countenance and saucy sense of humour. The leaves have been used in salads and the roots in stews especially during the Middle Ages.

It is very small right now though, and I think I have a few years to plan recipes for this one. It has a very subtle sweet taste that I can only compare to Butter Lettuce, which was one of my mom's garden standbys in the Canadian prairies.

Eastern Lemongrass is still alive after a couple of storms but is turning purple, so maybe it's too cold for it here.

Sweet Woodruff was wilted and dodgy at first, but thriving now with lots of new leaves. It is traditionally used in much German cooking: sausages, wackelpudding, ice cream, beers and wines. It has a vivid taste like no other, containing a strange chemical also found in cinnamon. I plan to make ice-cream and woodruff shortbread.

Chocolate Root or **Water Avens**. The blanched young leaves can be used in salads and the Elizabethans ground the dry root, producing a clove-like spice. It is also known as Indian Chocolate as Native Americans used to make a delicious drink from it. I plan to use the powdered root in Vanilla Bavarois and the leaves in a seafood cocktail.

Curry Plant is one of the few new arrivals I had tasted before. John and I ate lots of tasty bowls of fried curry leaves on spicy noodles during our foodie travels in Sri Lanka. It has an earthy curry taste. I will use it in our Massaman Curry Leaf and Peanut Sauce that we serve with our Mull-aged Venison Fillets and in my Paratha bread.

Wild Bergamot (Bee balm) is a sweet, fragrant plant and tastes like a cross between mint, oregano and Earl Grey tea. I plan to try it as a fresh-picked tea. We currently serve lemon balm and apple-mint teas on the menu. Jonny daringly dashes outside in his kilt during service, often in the rain, to pick them for our diners. When it blooms I also hope to use the petals in salad dressing.

The Losers

Pineapple Sage smells like pineapple and tastes very green, like grass. Not much like normal sage.

Black Peppermint is refreshing but disappointingly (for a chef with her gothic moments) not black!

Variegated Herb Gerard is a kind of ground elder (I googled it too late). We already have lots of unwanted elder rampaging on the croft. It tastes a bit like celery and can be used in soups and salads, and apparently 'super green smoothies', something that never sees the light of day in my hedonistic kitchen. I grow celery leaf and celtuce for this flavour profile already.

White Chives. Same problem as the Black Mint. Not white. Like normal chives; disappointing.

Lime Mint and **Grapefruit Mint** were a total loss, as they both seem to taste and smell, well . . . just like mint. I already have half an acre of it thanks to an over-zealous apple mint that broke the bounds of its pot 20 years ago (and is busy trying to thrash its way to Peebles).

My herb bed is also brimming with the usual culprits like thyme, sage, chives, dill, oregano, summer savory, nasturtiums and rosemary. There are still a few spots where I could possibly squish in another plant or two. Somewhere in the garden (I forget where) there are two black mulberries, and a couple of marshmallows and a few other things that I have failed to document. I am hoping some of my lottery winners flourish enough to be used in experiments in the Ninth Wave creative cauldron we call the kitchen. If not, I'm sure the ineffably Scottish husband will be on hand with soothing blandishments to help pick up the pieces.

BUCKWHEAT BLINI WITH GARDEN BEETROOT AND GOAT'S CHEESE

One of the all-time favourites on the Ninth Wave restaurant menu.
Serves 4

CHEESE TUILLES
60g/2oz Inverloch Goat's Cheese,
    roughly grated

BLINI MIX
200g/7oz buckwheat
1 shallot, diced
1 egg
2 tsp baking powder
300ml/10fl oz milk
2 tsp butter, melted
1 tsp dijon mustard
½ tsp sea salt
black pepper
8 small beetroot (4cm diameter)
buckwheat sprouts
rapeseed oil

GOAT'S CHEESE DRESSING
25g/1oz raw horseradish root
½ tsp granulated sugar
2 tsp white wine vinegar
150ml/5fl oz sour cream
30g/1oz Inverloch Goat's Cheese,
    finely grated

¼ tsp salt

Preheat oven to 180C/160C fan/350F/Gas 4.

Line a baking sheet with a non-stick silicon baking sheet. Sprinkle the grated cheese in roughly 3cm circles, 3cm apart on the sheet. Bake in the oven for 10 minutes until golden brown and crisp. Remove gently onto a cooling rack.

For the blini mix, beat all the ingredients well in a large bowl with a whisk. Place in a measuring jug. Cover and refrigerate.

Cut the leaves off the beetroot, leaving about 2cm of stem. Rinse the beets making sure that you don't disturb the skins.

Place the beets whole in a large pan of full of water and bring to the boil. Reduce the heat and simmer until tender for 20–30 minutes. The beetroot is cooked if the skin slides off when it is rubbed. Drain, cool and peel the beetroot. Cut into 1cm slices.

For the horseradish sauce, dissolve the salt and sugar in vinegar by stirring in a small bowl.

Peel the horseradish. Finely grate the horseradish into the vinegar. Add sour cream, cheese and whisk well. Chill.

Heat a large non-stick frying pan on medium heat. Grease lightly with oil. The pan is ready when small drops of water sizzle and disappear quickly.

Pour 6cm circles of batter spaced evenly around the

pan. Leave spaces in between the blinis so they remain separated. Cook 1 to 1½ minutes, turning with a fish slice (or flat spatula) when the edges look cooked and bubbles begin to break on the surface. Continue to cook for 1 to 1½ minutes or until golden brown. Keep the cooked blinis in a warm oven on a kitchen paper–lined plate.

Place one blini on each serving plate. Spread a teaspoon of horseradish sauce on each blini. Place three to four slices of beetroot on top. Place some buckwheat sprouts on top of the slices. Repeat. Top with the last blinis and garnish with the buckwheat sprouts. Serve immediately.

SPICED INVERLUSSA MUSSELS WITH BABY GARDEN CARROTS

This is a variation on a spicy Portuguese cream of carrot soup that I discovered on vacation. This recipe shows off our award-winning local mussels as well as utilizing tasty thinnings from the carrot patch.

Serves 4

1 large pinch of saffron threads
1 tbsp rapeseed oil
1 large carrot peeled and grated
12 baby carrots
3 shallots, finely sliced
1 garlic clove, crushed
150ml/5fl oz dry white wine
50ml/1½fl oz white vermouth
1kg/2lb 4oz cleaned mussels, de-
    bearded and rinsed
1 tsp flour
¼ tsp each of dry ground
    coriander, cumin and ginger
pinch of chilli powder
250ml/10fl oz double cream
½ tsp nam pla (fish sauce)
2 tbsp fresh coriander, roughly
    chopped
sea salt to taste

Place two tablespoons of boiling water over the saffron threads and set aside.

Boil a small pot of water on the stove and add the baby carrots. Cook for 3 to 5 minutes or until the carrots are just tender. Drain and set aside.

Heat the oil in a large saucepan with a tight-fitting lid. Cook the grated carrot, shallots and garlic on a gentle heat until soft but not coloured. Add the vermouth and wine and bring to the boil, then simmer for 4 minutes. Mix in the mussels and cover with the lid. Cook for 3 minutes.

Make sure that the cooked mussels are open. Drain into a colander placed over a large bowl. Discard any mussels that are still closed. Place the mussels in a covered bowl to keep warm. Strain the mussel liquor through muslin to remove the sediment. Pour the liquor into a clean pan. Simmer the mussel liquor for 7 to 9 minutes to reduce the volume by half.

Mix the flour and ginger, ground coriander, cumin and chilli powder together in a bowl. Slowly add the cream while whisking to blend. Add the saffron and its water to this mix. Add the spiced cream, baby carrots and fish sauce to the pan with the mussel liquor, stir and bring to a simmer. Season with salt.

Stir in the mussels and serve in bowls, garnished with the chopped coriander.

Note: Before cooking, discard any mussels that don't close when tapped, or are damaged.

BOGLED TATTIES AND GARDEN HORSERADISH WITH FRESH MACKEREL

Sweet, creamy-fleshed new potatoes contrast with the crispy mackerel skin of the seared mackerel fillets to produce the ultimate comfort dish. The horseradish and dill add shape and herbaceous notes to this symphony of taste.

Serves 4

8 mackerel fillets (pin bones
 removed)
1 tsp dill, finely chopped
2 tbsp rapeseed oil
4 tbsp plain flour
¼ tsp sea salt
black pepper
30g/1oz broad bean or pea shoots
 to garnish
2 sprigs dill for garnish

BOGLED TATTIES
80g/3oz garden broad beans
480g/1lb new potatoes, cooked
 with skin on
2 tbsp rapeseed oil
2 tbsp sour cream
2 tbsp fresh horseradish, grated
1 large shallot, minced
1 tsp sugar dissolved in 1 tsp white
 wine vinegar
1 tbsp spring onion, finely chopped
sea salt and black pepper to taste

Blanch the baby broad beans in a pan of salted boiling water for 1 minute. Drain and peel off the outer skin if desired.

For the potatoes, bring a large pan of salted water to the boil and boil the washed potatoes for 10 to 15 minutes, or until tender. Drain. When cooled slightly, cut them into quarters. Transfer the potatoes to a mixing bowl. Stir in the sour cream, vinegar, horseradish, shallots and broad beans and season to taste with salt and pepper.

For the mackerel, diagonally score the skin three times on each fillet. This will keep the skin from shrinking too much when searing. Rub the mackerel fillets with the chopped dill. On a plate, mix the flour, salt and a few twists of ground black pepper together. Coat the mackerel fillets all over in the seasoned flour. Shake off the excess flour.

In a very large frying pan, heat the rapeseed oil on medium high and place the mackerel fillets skin-side down. Fry until the skin is crispy and the fillets move easily in the pan, about 2 minutes. Turn over and fry for 1 to 2 minutes until the fish is just opaque.

Divide the bogled tatties between four warmed dinner plates and top with the pan-seared mackerel fillets. Garnish with dill and broad bean shoots.

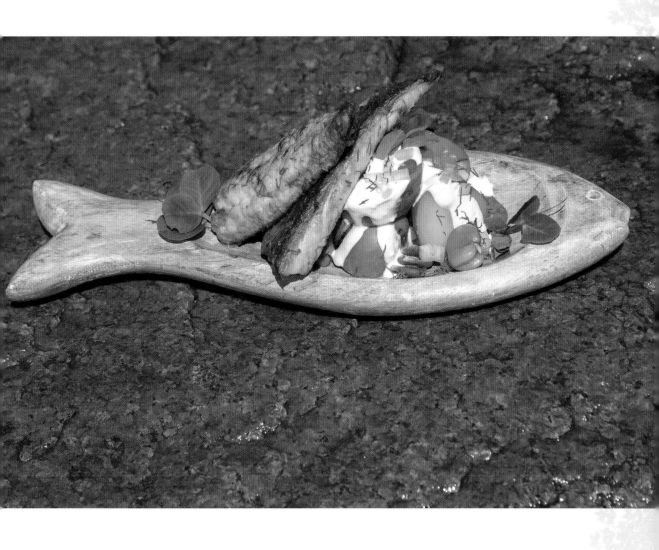

BEASTIES AND SUCH

Whether it is because of the climate, the miles of rough-hewn wilderness or the good clean air and clear waters, the meat and game on the Isle of Mull are second to none.

The Isle of Mull is an unfolding array of habitats and landscapes; from woodlands and bogs to wind-scoured basalt mountains, sea cliffs, and sandy beaches. The eagles and red deer tend to get most of the press here, but there is a marvellous larder available to the adventurous chef. Pheasant, Duck, Woodcock, Snipe, Pigeon, Geese, Widgeon, Rabbit, Brown Hare and Mountain Hare are all good eating. Venison, however, proves to be the most popular wild game on Mull menus.

Venison

The largest and most majestic animal to be found on Mull is the red deer. Red deer have graced the Mull landscape since Mesolithic times and play an integral part on our seasonal menu. It is a healthy option with low cholesterol and lean meat, offering great flavour and texture. We prefer a light ageing technique, and as a result the end product is less gamey than your average venison. We have converted many venison-virgins in the dining room. Aging the meat is also what tenderises it. We strike a fine balance between texture and taste, and our venison fillet is so tender it can usually be cut with a spoon. Marinated venison (as with any meat) also makes for a melt in the mouth product. I often use my bramble and nasturtium bud vinegar in the teriyaki marinade instead of rice vinegar. Steaks and fillets cook in minutes, and because of its low fat content, the meat doesn't shrink on cooking.

Because of Bambi's popularity many people regard hunting deer as cruel. The reality is that the red deer on Mull have reached a record-breaking population. Because they are not managed vigorously enough or sufficiently culled, the island cannot sustain the deer population, hence starvation in winter months is inevitable for some. Mindful stalkers take the beasts that will not make it through the winter and leave the king stags and healthy hinds to improve the breeding population.

Knock, Gruline and Lochbuie play home to the island's fallow deer. The fallow deer is between the roe and red in size, and is a grazing deer. It eats a wide range of plants and grasses. Fallow deer has a very bold, robust flavour with depth, and is often accompanied by juniper berries and wine marinades. It would go nicely in my recipe for Oatmeal-crusted Venison Loin with Roasted Autumn Beetroot and a Loganberry and Elderflower Rosé Glaze. It is believed that 6,000 of these creatures have come to inhabit the hills, woodlands and heath lands of Mull after they were introduced during Norman times.

One of the tastiest and often the chef's choice for venison game is the roe deer. Roe is a browsing deer, eating a wide variety of herbage and tree shoots which is evident in the sweet delicate flavour of the meat. It is a smaller species of deer that is choosy about its food. It is said only to eat the most succulent and fragrant leaves in the wild. The perfect accompaniments to this wonderful meat are wild edible shoots and herbs that have been foraged near where the deer live; wood sorrel, sheep sorrel, clover, ramson, primroses and pink purslane to name a few. It is best served as carpaccio, scattered with these wild foods, or cooked and served with fresh garden vegetables and a light jus that will not overpower it. Unlike other game, roe deer can be taken almost all year round including the spring (1 April to 31 October for bucks, 1 November to 31 March for does).

Every winter the local red deer decide that the vegetable garden and our ornamental shrubbery that we've toiled to create are tasty winter fodder. Jonny says he has to disabuse them of this notion in the only language they can possibly understand. One year Jonny took three deer for our freezer, but only after they'd eaten our entire crop of broccoli, cabbage, leeks and lettuce. That was before we put the deer fence up. When I moved here 20 years ago, deer never ventured this far along the Ross and no extra fencing was needed.

Jonny had gone out early on a windy January morning to find the culprits which had been decimating my hydrangeas, lilacs and buddleia bushes. He'd managed to find the deer at the top end of the croft. He could see them against the dawn sky and dropped a male that was past its breeding prime. It was a heavy beast and Jonny needed help getting it over a section of sheep fence. I was useless for such a task, so he asked a friend to help. Even then it was quite an undertaking. They were trying to flip the stag end for end over the fence, when the antlers caught on the wire and the carcase was catapulted backwards. One of the hoofs caught Jonny right in the middle of his forehead and showered him with glaur. John's helper laughed and said, 'He got you pretty good there!' Sporting a hoof print on his face, Jonny dusted himself off and replied, 'Not as good as I got him!'

That beast supplied a lot of tasty venison which was honestly appreciated by many. We like to share our largesse, so after butchering, Jonny distributed venison mince, stewing meat and roasts amongst many happy villagers.

Beef

A loveable symbol of the Scottish northlands, Highland cattle can be seen all over Mull. Capable of thriving in the harshest environmental conditions of the rough hill country of Scotland, Highland cattle are tough. The breed is widely considered to be the hardiest breed of cattle to be found anywhere in the world. The meat is very lean with a well rounded flavour. Aside from producing world class beef, Highland cattle are also used for habitat conservation in heather moor land regeneration, as their grazing habits can assist wildlife and biodiversity. They stamp down unwanted bracken and brambles. Using their long sturdy horns, they dauntlessly clear their way through the thickest of

scrub and undergrowth, foraging as they go. The grasses and wildflowers naturally regenerate as a result of their clearing.

We use Ardalanish Highland beef. Ardalanish Farm is renowned for its organic methods and traditional cattle breeds. It lies in the south west corner of Mull, where they also rear native Kyloe cattle. The Kyloe's grazing patterns are like those of wild herbivores, copying the activities of the extinct wild aurochs (prehistoric oxen).

Although the cattle are slow to mature, the meat is very tender and tends to be much leaner than most beef, as the thick shaggy coat supplies the majority of the animal's insulation, rather than fat. The meat from these grass-fed cows is lean and well marbled and reasonably low in fat and cholesterol.

Their Highland cows feast on the succulent shoots of weeds and blooms in the spring, which enriches the sweet taste of the meat. Cattle are allowed to range freely and mature naturally. Feeding on the heather-clad hills, as well as browsing the Hebridean coastline for seaweed, give the beef a unique taste profile. In winter when ground cover is sparse, cattle are fed home-grown organic fodder. The cattle are slaughtered locally and the meat hung for three to four weeks before being handled by the Isle of Mull Community butcher.

Lamb

The unique grazing combination of heather, mosses, grasses and seaweed give Mull lamb a truly unique flavour. Many crofts and much common grazing land include tidal flats, beaches or shoreline.

On Mull, we believe there is a link between a wholesome landscape and the highest quality meat. The flavour of the island lamb and mutton echoes the land itself because the two are so tightly bound together. Their diet of wild grasses, heather and the berries, eaten amidst our unspoilt island landscape, makes for a great product. Ewes which are able to forage on the shore enrich their diet with seaweed during the winter months when they are pregnant

and just after lambing. Slow growth on a diet of grasses and wild plants also reduces shrinkage in the pan during cooking,

We get the lamb from several crofts, including nearby Knockvologan Farm run by locals John and Linda Cameron. Knockvologan lamb racks have a sweet taste with a modest fat cap to ensure a moist meat. Ninth Wave is lucky enough to obtain a few of these choice racks once or twice a year.

We also do business with the award winning Treshnish Farm on the rugged north-west coast of the island. The Charringtons came to Treshnish Farm in 1994, where they have since improved the different habitats on the farm for both wildlife and livestock.

In 2011 the farm won the UK RSPB Nature of Farming Award for wildlife-friendly farming. In the summer months you can watch the sheep graze in the fields that are ablaze with wild flowers. Their slowly matured lamb tastes especially good because they graze in these traditional meadows filled with delicious herbage and wild flowers, coastal heath land and extensive open hill, giving them a varied natural diet. Having a slaughterhouse on the island reduces the stress for the animals and a small personalised set up allows them to ensure the beasts are carefully hung and butchered.

We buy tasty Blackface wedder (male sheep of two years of age) from Treshnish. Because they are naturally reared and not intensively fed, the animal takes longer to get to a good size for butchering, so becomes a wedder rather than a lamb. Luckily, the more mature they are, the richer the flavour.

Eggs

We use small hen's eggs from the pullets and rare breed chickens at Ardfenaig. We also use hen and duck eggs from a neighbouring croft. When going to pick up eggs from Sandra down the Kintra road, I drive up to the house and am greeted by a dozen ducks, chickens, two smiling children and an enthusiastic Rhodesian ridgeback the size of a horse. We love her free-range eggs and use them for everything from our breakfast fry-ups to Earl Grey gateaux, ice creams and crab soufflés.

THE CHICKEN LADY

The lady who lives at nearby Ardfenaig House has become known fondly as Anne the Chicken lady. She treats her chickens as house guests who have free rein to roam her grand entrance hall and drawing room. Her chickens are a strange bunch, from silkies, to punk-rock haired Appenzeller-Spitzhauben Silver Spangled and Orpington Jubilee hens.

They also come with personal monikers such as Beulah, Beauregarde, Marge and Howard. Once Anne even came into the village shop with a live hen in her handbag. I always make sure to ask after Howard as he seems to be quite a character. One day I ran into Anne (sans poulet) in Bunessan and asked how Howard was. Anne said in her treacle-slow Georgian drawl 'Hawrd's head looks laike it's bin throo a meat griin-der. The other fellas are just pickin' on him cause he likes the ladies so much!' I answered jokingly, 'Maybe you could get him a little helmet or something?' and Anne said, 'Yeah I could make it to match his diaper. You could dress it down for daytime or dress it up for evening.'

Most of Anne's eggs are halfway in size between a small hen's egg and a quail's egg. Opening a pink box of these eggs is like opening a box of crayons – perfection in an array of pastel shades from eau-de-nil to peach. I use these wee beauties poached on top of our Smoked Haddock and Oriental Mushroom Consommé and basted on our Highland Beef Fillet Fry-up on the brunch menu.

Sandra produces more duck eggs than hen's eggs. Her White Runner ducks lay eggs that are large and full of flavour. You can eat them in the same way as hen's eggs and they are also great for baking with. Duck eggs also have a larger yolk to white ratio which I prefer in a breakfast egg. The result is richer, smoother scrambled, fried or poached eggs.

When using duck eggs your baked goods will be richer, moister and fluffier. Farmers in Saskatchewan often used duck eggs for baking when I was growing up in the prairies and I can still remember how superior those cakes and corn biscuits tasted.

Pork

We also get pork from Sandra. She was very relieved to turn her porkers into sausages this time around, as they'd been the most troublesome pigs she'd ever had. A pig lover by nature, Sandra should have known these were mischief-

DUCKIES

- Duck eggs have more protein and contain twice the amount of iron and five times the amount of Vitamin B-12 as chicken eggs.
- They can differ in taste from one breed of duck to another.
- Duck eggs contain more calories, fat, dietary cholesterol and healthy omega 3 fatty acids than chicken eggs.
- Because duck eggs have a more robust shell than hen's eggs they are said to keep longer in storage.
- Boiling: for soft-boiled (average-sized duck egg) 6 to 7 minutes; for hard-boiled, 9 minutes.

makers when she'd first gone to buy them from an estate in Pennyghael, only to find they had escaped and were running down the single track road towards Craignure.

Many a time last summer she'd phone up to say, 'If ye see any of my piggies, give me a call. It's the fourth time this week!' They'd escaped through the drainage pipe this time and were headed over our way. Everyone in the village knew the piggy band by sight. One stripy one, two black and a speckled one. Not that there were that many rogue groups of swine roaming the area. So far they'd been captured in a cattle barn four miles away, caught eating the neighbour's hen feed at their back door, lounging in front of the village shop and down at Tor Mor beach enjoying the sun. They even knew how to wait for a really rainy day when they would gang up to hike the fence posts right out of the mud to escape from their pen. Anyway, they eventually made for very tasty sausages, which amazingly stayed in the pan.

Isle of Mull also has other quality organic pork producers. Sgriob Ruadh Farm near Tobermory has in recent years begun to produce pork and Ony Boa's hand-reared pork near Dervaig is known for well-flavoured meat. These pigs live outside in fields and meadows and feed naturally on wild plants. Jonny and I yearly buy a pig carcass, usually Gloucester Old Spot, and turn it into all manner of tasty things. I particularly enjoy making and curing my own spicy chorizo sausages. I also love using the pork mince in Japanese Gyosa dumplings.

On an island of such natural resources it's not surprising that we have a great group of quality food producers and suppliers. We believe in slow food principles and using what this exquisite island has to offer.

From smoked fish, to hand-dived scallops, from award-winning cheeses to Highland beef, from lamb to wild sea trout, the Isle of Mull has plenty to entice. A list of local suppliers can be found at the back of this book.

Cheese
Old Scots *Kebbuck*, Gaelic *Cais*

Tangy, full-bodied, evocative: Scotland produces some of the best cheeses in the world. There are currently over two dozen cheese makers in Scotland. Our after-dinner cheeseboard features a true cross-section of what the artisan cheesemakers of the Celtic north have to offer. Special mention goes to the award-winning Isle of Mull cheeses, as they are so very good and so very local and are deservedly the stars of our cheeseboard.

We offer five cheeses at a time and change the line-up depending on time of year and availability. We serve them with handmade oatcakes and our Bramble and Beetroot Chutney, and this year Tweedside Wildflower Raw Honeycomb will also be featured. Below is a bit of information about our favourite cheeses.

Isle of Mull Cheddar is traditional unpasteurized farmhouse cheddar from Tobermory. Isle of Mull Cheddar is considered by many to be the king of Scottish cheddars. Cheese maker Brendan Reade describes it as strong, peaty and herby with fruity notes. He also adds that overtones of fruit and whisky are due to the cows often feeding on the remains of fermented grain from the nearby Tobermory malt distillery. Mull cheddar is a complex cheese that echoes the many facets of the island landscape in which it is made.

Isle of Mull Hebridean Blue is a creamy, well-rounded cheese, handmade from natural raw cow's milk and aged for twelve weeks. It is tangy and delicate with a deep, dark flavour and a magical aftertaste that speaks of the sea. This cheese has taken the Best Blue Cheese in Britain award. It is the only blue cheese made in the Hebrides.

Black Gruth Dubh Crowdie is made in the Highlands. Gruth Dubh is a soft, tangy cheese that is rolled in pinhead oatmeal and crushed black peppercorns. It is made from mid-fat cow's milk by the Stone family in Tain. Crowdie was thought to have been brought to Scotland by the Vikings in the eighth century and is akin to cottage cheese. I love this cheese's contrasts; creamy yet zesty, fruity yet hot and spicy from the pepper. I eat this by itself, in a room by myself, so I don't have to share.

Dunsyre Blue is a mould-ripened, handmade cheese that comes from Lanarkshire and is crafted by H.J. Errington. It has a deep, lusty flavour and is made using the rich, unpasteurized milk of Ayrshire cows. It is soft and creamy and goes well with roasted figs or pear tart tatin.

Clava is an organic brie-style cheese made by Connage Dairy at Ardersier. Clava brie is an inviting and mild cheese if eaten early on. If left to ripen for 6-8 weeks until soft and silky its earthy nuttiness and unique clover flavours are brought to light.

Inverloch Goat's Cheese is a flavourful but a less gamey tasting goat's cheese which is subtle on the palate. It is made in Campbeltown on the Mull of Kintyre with 100% pasteurized goat's milk. Crafted using no animal rennet, it is great for vegetarians and is an award-winner with a fine texture and waxed rind. Classy and not overpowering.

Other Favourites

Iona Cromag, a winning number from the Reades on the Isle of Mull. It is a washed curd cheese and made using unpasteurized ewe's milk and vegetarian rennet. The rind is washed in Iona whisky from the Tobermory Distillery. This semi-soft, seasonal treat has a medium texture and a mild taste with mushroom undertones.

Captain's Claret is another offering from Inverloch Cheese Company. An unusual, ballsy cheese veined with rich Bordeaux wine. Creamy with tart yet earthy undertones. You either love it or hate it. Goes well with a tankard of full-bodied red.

Bishop Kennedy originated from the medieval monasteries in France and is named after a fifteenth-century bishop of St Andrews. Bishop Kennedy is a soft, brie-like cheese produced by Kinfauns Home Farm in Perthshire. The rind is washed with brine and whisky during its eight-week maturation, which gives it its unique orangey-red skin. When ripened fully this cheese has a smooth, runny texture with a heady aroma and sultry, earthy undertones.

Strathdon Blue is a hedonistic, full-fat blue cheese made by Ruaraidh Stone near Tain, Ross-shire, in his dairy which is housed in an old seaside brewery. This is a super-satisfying cheese on so many levels. One taste opens a treasure-trove of contrasting notes with an evocative saltiness on the finish. Great with fresh bread or bannocks.

Grimbister is a traditional Orkney farmhouse cheese made to a secret family recipe handed down through the generations. It is made from unpasteurized cows' milk and can be eaten early on (from six weeks) but we prefer it aged for another 4 weeks or so. When young it is pleasant, smooth and mild. When aged further, a long lemony taste develops and the cheese turns slightly crumbly. Works perfectly with wild berries or a good chenin blanc.

Mull's Own: More about Isle of Mull Cheese

In 1981 Jeff and Christine Reade moved to Sgriob-ruadh Farm (pronounced 'Ski-brooah', and meaning 'red furrow') just outside Tobermory. Over thirty years later, what began as a roofless ruin is a neat farmhouse and a bustling

array of farm buildings. This is Mull's only dairy farm and we are very proud of all the awards they have deservedly won and their green approach to business.

They strive to keep their cheese as natural as possible, and add no colouring. For that reason, their winter cheeses, made when the cows are hay-fed, are whiter in appearance than those made when the cattle are fed on fresh, green grass. The cheeses are commended for their individuality of flavour and taste. Sgriob-ruadh avoids pasteurisation, seeing it as an aggressive treatment that destroys many of the friendly organisms in cheese which give them their unique flavour profiles.

Their raw cheeses are made from Sgriob-ruadh milk. The cows are milked in the morning and the milk is taken directly from the parlour to the cheese-making vat. The results are their famous Isle of Mull, Hebridean Blue, Iona Cromag and a number of variants with additions such as cranberry, garlic and mustard. Visitors can often see the cheese-making process under way and view the maturing stash of cheeses in the purpose-built cellar. There is a wee farm shop where you can purchase cheese or a wonderful glasshouse (made out of the timbers of an old village hall) where you can stop for a cuppa.

We use their cheeses in our Stuffed Courgette Blossoms, our Sea Urchin and Red Onion Bisque, Cheddar and Caraway Tuilles and Cheesy Oatcakes.

WILD VENISON CARPACCIO WITH PICKLED GINGER AND GREENS

This recipe was adapted from a beef dish I ate in a Chinatown diner. Fresh venison has an even more complex flavour profile than beef and is especially good with our homemade pickled ginger.

Serves 4

450g/1lb venison loin steak, in one
    piece (start a day ahead)
1 tsp vegetable oil

VENISON MARINADE
125ml/4fl oz soy sauce
60ml/2fl oz sake or mirin
2 tbsp light brown sugar
2 cloves garlic, minced
1 tbsp minced fresh ginger
½ small onion
120ml/4fl oz mandarin (or fresh
    orange) juice
black pepper

SALAD
200g/7oz mixed leaves (rocket,
    mizuna, mibuna)
2 tbsp cress or bean sprouts
30g/1oz bamboo shoots, julienned
30g/1oz red pepper, julienned
30g/1oz yellow pepper, julienned
petals from 1 marigold
petals from 4 primroses
40g/1½oz gari (pickled ginger)

MANDARIN AND SESAME
    DRESSING
zest and juice of 1 mandarin orange
60ml/2 fl oz rice wine vinegar
¼ tsp powdered ginger
1 tbsp dark soy
10ml/½fl oz sesame oil
4 Sichuan peppercorns crushed
½ clove garlic, minced
½ tsp honey

TO SERVE
a dot of wasabi paste
20g/¾oz sesame seeds

To make the marinade, blend all the ingredients in the food processor. Submerge the trimmed venison loin in the marinade, cover and refrigerate overnight. If the venison is not completely covered in the marinade you will have to turn it so all sides are equally marinated.

Wipe off the venison loin. Reserve the marinade. Heat oil in a frying pan on medium high until very hot. Sear the venison loin on each side (it is a cylinder, so roll it over three times to cook it all) for 3 minutes. Remove from the heat and submerge the venison in the marinade once more. Let it cool. Cover and refrigerate for 4-7 hours. You can remove the venison from the marinade at this point and keep the meat well wrapped in the fridge. It will keep for 24 hours if you'd like to make it a day ahead.

Make the dressing by blending all the ingredients with a whisk or hand-blender.

Just before you are ready to serve, dry the venison off and thinly slice the cylinder into rounds 3-4mm thick.

Place four serving plates at the ready. Mix the salad ingredients together and place a line of salad down one half of each plate. Fan one quarter of the venison slices on each plate. Place a dot of wasabi (hot Japanese horseradish) on each plate. Put dressing on the salad and garnish the plate with flower petals, sesame seeds and gari.

157

HIGHLAND BEEF FILLET WITH CELTUCE SAUCE AND PIGNUTS

The intense flavour of Highland beef plays excellently against the verdant taste of the herb celtuce and the earthiness of Hebridean blue cheese. The fresh pignuts add a nutty, sweet taste and crunchy texture. Raw celeriac or macadamia nuts could be substituted.

Serves 4

500g/1lb 2oz fillet of Ardalanish beef
1 tbsp vegetable oil
120g/4oz Isle of Mull Hebridean Blue Cheese
80g/3oz pignuts, cleaned
8 sprigs celtuce

CELTUCE SAUCE
25g/1oz butter
25g/1oz plain flour
300ml/10fl oz white veal stock or chicken stock
300ml/10fl oz single cream
60ml/2fl oz white wine
2 tbsp chopped shallots
3 tbsp chopped celtuce (or celery leaf)
1 tbsp parsley
2 pinches celery salt
sea salt and white pepper to taste

In a heavy-bottomed saucepan, fry the shallots in 25g/1oz of butter on low until translucent. With a wooden spoon, stir the flour into the melted butter a little bit at a time, until it is fully incorporated into the butter, giving you a pale yellow paste. Heat this roux for another minute or so to cook off the taste of raw flour. Using a whisk, slowly add the cool veal stock to the roux, whisking vigorously to remove any lumps. Add the cream, celery salt, parsley and celtuce, then lower the heat to a simmer and reduce for about 5 minutes.

Season to taste with sea salt and white pepper. Blend until smooth with a hand blender.

Cut the beef fillet into four equal-sized steaks. Heat a griddle or cast-iron frying pan until smoking hot. Season the steaks with sea salt and black pepper. Coat the steaks in vegetable oil. Sear the fillet on all sides in the pan for 3 to 4 minutes per side, then place on a board, covered, in a warm place and leave to rest for 5 to 7 minutes.

To serve, place the steaks on serving plates with a portion of the celtuce sauce. Garnish each with 40g blue cheese and sprigs of celtuce (or celery leaf) and pignuts.

TRESHNISH RACK OF LAMB PERSIAN-STYLE WITH JEWELLED RICE

The middle-eastern ingredients in this recipe make our local free-range lamb sing.
Note: here the bitter taste of hogweed seeds (never to be confused with poisonous giant hogweed) add that authentic Persian taste profile, but ground fennel seeds can be used as a substitute.

2 racks of Treshnish lamb, French-trimmed
4 tbsp pomegranate seeds

FOR THE JEWELLED RICE:
250g/9oz basmati rice
500ml/16fl oz water
¼ tsp salt
60g/2oz barberries (or dried cranberries)
1 tsp butter
¼ tsp saffron threads
pinch of sugar
2 pinches of dried rose petals

FOR THE GOLPAR PASTE
    (a Persian take on pesto):
2 tbsp fresh coriander, chopped
2 tbsp mint, chopped
2 tbsp Asian basil, chopped
1 small clove of garlic, minced
1 tbsp pomegranate molasses
1 tsp agave syrup or honey
40g/1½oz walnuts, chopped
½ tsp ground Golpar (hogweed seeds) or ground fennel seeds
sea salt and black pepper to taste

FOR THE SPINACH
    BOORANIYEH
    (a creamy yoghurt and garlic dip):
60g/2oz (½ small) sweet white onion
1 tbsp olive oil
1 garlic clove, very thinly sliced
325g/11oz fresh spinach, washed
125ml/4fl oz yoghurt
125ml/4fl oz sour cream
½ tsp sea salt
black pepper

To make the golpar paste, put the herbs, garlic and walnuts in a mortar and pestle and grind to combine. Add other ingredients and mix well. Season to taste.

To make the spinach dip, steam the spinach for 3 minutes, allow to cool. Fry the onions in a dash of olive oil in a frying pan on low heat until translucent. Add the garlic into the onions to cook for a further minute. Cool. Add the onions and garlic into the yoghurt, add the sea salt and black pepper and mix well. Squeeze any water from the spinach and chop. Add the spinach to the yoghurt and mix well.

Preheat the oven to 220C/200C fan/425F/Gas 7.

Isle of Mull lamb is very lean. If you are using a fatty lamb rack, the fat cap must either be rendered, fat down in a frying pan on low until most of the fat is melted off, or trimmed off to a suitable thickness.

Score the fat lightly in a criss-cross pattern, but without cutting through to the meat.

Place the lamb in a roasting tray and spread a generous tablespoon of golpar paste over the entire lamb rack, working it into the meat and score lines.

Roast for 15 minutes for rare, 20 minutes for medium-rare. After 10 minutes, cover the rack with a sheet of tin foil to prevent the molasses paste from burning.

Meanwhile, prepare the rice. Rinse the rice in cold water and place in a small pot with 500ml water, the saffron, butter, salt, sugar, rose petals and barberries. Bring to the boil, stir, then cover and turn the heat to low. Cook 10 to 12 minutes.

Remove the pan from the heat, still covered, and stand for 3 minutes.

Once the lamb is cooked, leave the meat to rest, covered, in a warm place for 5 to 7 minutes. Carve it by cutting through the meat between the bones to give each person two or three cutlets (depending on the cutlet size). Spoon the rice onto warmed plates and arrange the lamb cutlets on top. Garnish with a teaspoonful of spinach booraniyeh, a teaspoon of golpar mix, and a sprinkling of pomegranate seeds and rose petals.

HOISIN GLAZED MULL PORK BELLY WITH SWEET WOODRUFF AND BOK CHOY

Mull free-range pork is so flavourful in this recipe. The delicious fat bastes the meat by itself and ends up wonderfully caramelized and tender. We use sweet woodruff to impart a decidedly spicy aspect to the pork, but you can use cinnamon instead. The pork is possibly even better when reheated as leftovers.

Serves 4

1 kg/2lb 4oz pork belly
1 tbsp sweet woodruff leaves or ¼
    tsp cinnamon
1 tbsp honey
1 tsp five-spice powder
2 tbsp vegetable oil
5 cloves garlic, minced
2 tbsp grated palm sugar or brown
    sugar
4 tbsp dark soy sauce
3 star anise
6 shallots, finely chopped
260ml/9fl oz pork stock
1 tsp sea salt
4 heads bok choy

Using a very sharp knife, slice the pork into strips about 1.5cm thick. Do not remove the skin or fat which will become yummy and unctuous when cooked. Mix one tablespoon of the soy sauce with the woodruff, honey and five-spice powder in a bowl, and marinade the sliced pork in the mixture for 1 to 3 hours in the fridge.

Heat the oil to a high temperature in a heavy-bottomed pan with a well-fitting lid. Fry the garlic, shallots, star anise and sugar together until they begin to turn gold. Turn the heat down to medium and add the pork and marinade to the pan. Fry the pork until it is browned on all sides.

Add the stock, salt and the rest of the soy sauce. Bring the mix to the boil, reduce to a gentle simmer, cover and continue to simmer for two hours, turning the meat regularly. Add a little water to the pan if the sauce seems to be reducing and thickening too much.

Just before serving, cut the bok choy in half and steam for 2 minutes. Serve on warmed plates with the pork belly. Garnish with spring onions, sweet woodruff or clover flowers.

DROPPING MYSELF IN IT: THE QUEST FOR IMPROVEMENT

We are happy doing what we do and plan to keep it up. We will continue to better ourselves, supplementing our knowledge with further education and our inspirational foodie tours in the winter months whenever possible. However, once in a while my desire to improve myself and broaden the kitchen's culinary horizons doesn't go quite to plan.

Macarons: Another Kitchen Experiment

I knew that macarons wouldn't be easy. Rarely do chefs master these French fancies on the first or second go. What lunacy drew me to this egregious variety of meringue? The technical difficulty involved and the fact that the rest of the planet seems gaga about them would usually be enough to put me off. But there is something about their bright rainbow colours, their symmetry and their decadence. I was always mesmerized by a perfectly glorious box of crayons in all its splendour when I was a kid. I believe it was this memory that overrode my common sense. After all, I had more pleasant tasks to do before the restaurant opened for the spring: repair the gaping holes in the road, weed the evil rosebay willowherb, nettles and yarrow from the garden in a storm, or hand-strip and re-varnish the entire dining room floor.

Macarons it was then. A delicate confectionery for those with a true sweet tooth, the macaron is made with egg whites, icing sugar, granulated sugar, ground almonds and food colouring. The macaron can be filled with butter-cream or jam filling sandwiched between two rounds.

I was prepared: four day-old egg whites at the ready, twice-sifted ground almonds weighed out digitally to a fine decimal point, work stations pristine.

Me and kitchen assistant Fédra had our squeaky-clean utensils and powdered flavourings at the ready. I was unusually nervous. A new frontier. I said to Fédra as we weighed out the ingredients a third time, 'This is supposed to be fun isn't it? This isn't fun yet.'

She just smiled kindly, handed me my frilled holly-print apron (a prize from the village hall Christmas raffle) and made me a cup of PG Tips. I felt more like a cross between Laura Ashley and Vincent Price in *The Abominable Dr Phibes* than I did a chef. (All the photos of my attire that day have mysteriously vanished as the result of a computer glitch.)

FÉDRA

Macarons debatably originated in 1533 from one of *Catherine de' Medici's* Italian pastry chefs when she was brought to France to marry the king. Their name is derived from an Italian word *maccherone* (originally *ammaccare*) meaning to crush, which probably refers to the ground almond paste which is the main component. Although the ingredients are simple, the macaron batter has to be exactly the right consistency. A good macaron is defined by its smooth, domed top, ruffled base (referred to as the 'foot'), and flat bottom. The outer shell is supposed to be thin and crisp, and the whole creation made to melt away in the mouth.

I'd swotted for this experiment. I'd read every article I could find on the subject and watched numerous *how to* and *how not to* videos on YouTube until I was beating egg whites in my sleep (poor Jonny's hairdo was quite something when he woke up *that* morning. Don King move over!)

Fédra and I measured, beat, added, beat, coloured, beat and mixed to the letter of the recipe. We were both silent, concentrating, holding our breath.

I had decided that I would try to make three different kinds at once. Foolish girl. I also decided, in my wisdom, that although macarons never have flavourings in the batter itself, that I would go against almost 500 years of tradition and add flavours to the mix. I realized that added moisture was the probable danger factor. Incorporating dry flavours into meringue mix should work.

For our three flavours (one sweet and two savoury) we had freeze-dried raspberry powder, dried beetroot powder and green Thai curry spices.

The first problem was when we divided the mixture into three parts before mixing in the tasty powders. One third of our mixture was a very small amount and it was really difficult to fold things into it without losing all the air in the egg whites. We persevered and piped the finished mixes onto our baking tray lined with parchment paper.

After drying them at room temperature for an hour, banging the trays hard on the counter as per instructions, I cooked them at 160C. In videos they said if your macarons didn't peel off the paper neatly with nothing left behind, then they weren't done. 10 to 12 minutes was supposed to do it.

OK. 10 minutes – no chance, messy and the paper not peeling off. 12 minutes – not a hope. 20 minutes – Aargh! Again Fédra kindly smiled at me, with a tinge of pity this time. 30 minutes? NO.

Now they were starting to brown and there was no way this had worked. Upon close inspection, they looked ok . . . not cracked, not too puffy, smooth as a maiden's cheek. But try as we might, we also concluded that the paper was *never* going to come off. The reason? I'd somehow got non-stick baking parchment mixed up with the white tissue-like paper that I used to pack cookies in at Christmas. Paper-filled macaron, anyone?

Disaster at the first go. That said, I think the flavour powders were a success. The texture seemed uncompromised and the look was right. The macarons even had perfect little ruffly feet.

So, it's a bit too early to invite the neighbours in for a macaron-tasting session, but at least Jonny has something interesting to dunk into his elevenses cuppa.

I'll just tell him it's edible rice paper.

(Fired with enthusiasm before the experiments I had insanely offered to make 360 mini-macarons for the local wedding of a wonderful girl, Alison. We eventually filled the order and they looked magical, but never, never again.)

Michelin Stars in My Eyes

I could have had a quiet winter: reading *A Day at elBulli* by the peat fire, leisurely concocting new recipes in my tiny kitchen while listening to the gales ravaging our croft, and feeding Jonny up to help him keep warm on his fishing boat . . .

It's easy to be happily out of the loop of the greater culinary world when you work in the magical back of beyond. But no. Aware of the dangers of coasting, stagnating or playing it too safe as a chef, I thought I'd go out on limb for the good of all.

I applied for, and was accepted to do a short *estage* at Gidleigh Hall in Devon. I had the privilege of working under the impressive, two Michelin-starred chef Michael Caines MBE. A big kitchen and an even bigger personality. Much to his credit he didn't even swear at me.

At first I felt dwarfed and daunted by the labyrinth of rooms brimming with up to seventeen chefs at a time. I bought a hat, safety shoes and pressed my chef jackets with military precision. I didn't mention the fact that I owned a restaurant. I was freaked out that they might think I knew how to do more than I did. I started at the bottom. I was wielding my wee paring knife like a gunslinger . . . peeling buckets of shallots and up to my oxters in heaps of naves (baby turnips) waiting to be trimmed. I was chastised, ever so nicely, for the chaos of my work-station and took pains to polish my space until I could see my glaikit expression reflected there.

Any readers who followed my Gidleigh adventure on the Ninth Wave Facebook page will remember my 'trial by geometric shapes'. Although I have worked in restaurants since the age of 14, I'm not classically trained, and have never had to carve perfect 6mm x 4mm rectangles out of leeks or fashion 5,000 perfect fennel cubes. After weeks of practice, I wouldn't say I was speedy, but had a good grasp on cubes and was looking forward to the challenges of doing cumquat parallelograms and lime dodecahedrons. I was grateful for the initiation into the sacred world of knife skills and was surprised my phalanges came out of it unscathed.

The real experience is *not* like the restaurant estages on Masterchef. I was once again gullible enough to believe that television is real. You are not there for a lesson, or to be taught how to make dishes. I was squished into a corner by the dish pit with a cutting board, and everybody was so busy they hardly had time to tell me anything. How much you learn is up to you. You have to be pushy, put yourself forward and extract what info you can. They thought I was shy (me, who once flew to London to perform a poem in a tutu and red-sequined Doc Martens, wielding a child's accordion). Most of the chefs were friendly and the youngest team member, Toby, and the head pastry chef, Andrew King, were especially good to me, taking the time to explain the Gidleigh way.

As part of a kitchen staff that often outnumbered the patrons four to one, I learned the secrets of impeccable garnishing with micro everything; mini red amaranth, matchstick julienne of Granny Smith apple, and chiffonade of peeled mange-tout. What I really needed was a magnifying glass and a pair of neuro-surgical tweezers. However, always a fan of intricate decoration, I loved this part. I was excited at the thought of putting my own twist on the new design ideas and techniques I had gleaned.

I came to Devon a *sous-vide* virgin, never even having heard of the space-age Thermomix machine (of which they had at least two, at £3,000 a pop). I learned how the big boys do things and got a taste of the Michelin game. I am thankful for the experience and intend to incorporate a few techniques and flourishes into my slow food menu at Ninth Wave.

But most of all I learned that it's O.K. to be small, to be different. I now know that I am in the right place, doing the right thing for me. I cook fresh food that I love to eat, in a way that is true to my ingredients, for lovely people who deserve all good things.

A Better Chocolate

I am on a never-ending search for the perfect Ninth Wave chocolate. Our chocolates are made with fresh ingredients from our croft and garden. I hand-make them in small batches so no manufactured ingredients need to be added to prolong shelf-life, unlike most chocolates. I use only fresh Scottish double cream, organic Scottish butter, Valrhona chocolate and fresh plants for flavouring.

Our flavours in dark 70% cocoa solid chocolate are: Sea salt and Seaweed, Sweet Woodruff and Espresso, Whin Blossom and Blaeberry and Beetroot. Our white chocolate choices are: Bramble and Drambuie Cranachan, Meadowsweet and Heather Honey, Rhubarb and Custard and Elderflower Rosé with Pink Peppercorns. Our Cranachan chocolates are by far the most popular. Cranachan is a traditional Scottish dessert made from whipped cream, soft fruit, Drambuie liqueur, toasted oatmeal, and honey. I designed the chocolate around this classic pudding. It contains two layers of ganache, one Drambuie flavoured and one fresh bramble puree and cream layer. It is then enrobed in white chocolate and topped with a stripe of dehydrated bramble powder and a crunchy oatmeal and honey nugget.

I started out making chocolates

THE CHOCOLATE-MAKER

169

in the dour bothy fifteen years ago for a Christmas produce fair. I had one single mould, no counter, no running hot water and no insulated walls. It was rustic to say the least. I remember moulding the last of the 1,130 chocolates that I'd made and sold that year. I was working on a DIY coffee table which was 18 inches off the ground and I was crawling around the floor wielding my palette knife like something from 'Return of the Mummy'. My back had seized up and I ended up with repetitive strain injury in my elbows and wrists. Dear Jonny came into the room, took pity on me and packaged the last chocolates for me. The things I do to myself for fun!

Over the years I've had quite a few escapades while trying to further my chocolate-making skills. One winter I thought I'd go and take a course from the renowned Slattery's Patissier and Chocolatier in Manchester. I made it all the way down there on public transport without a hitch and was looking forward to it. I walked into their professional school kitchen the next morning and met all the friendly people. As soon as the demonstration started I knew I was in trouble. Where was the introduction to different chocolates? The tempering demo? The gentle easing in of us beginners?

I was really in the poop, alright. It seems that I'd inadvertently signed up for an *advanced* master-class. We were about to learn how to construct five-foot tall chocolate centrepieces for professional competitions. Oh Jesus. I think I cried.

I was behind from the start. All the others had taken several Slattery courses already, including the beginners' basics that I thought I'd booked in for. I had that nauseating defeated feeling that I felt all during my early school days. I eventually finished the two-day workshop with only a handful of tantrums and a towering monstrosity of chocolatiness that was burgeoning with abstract shapes, sculpted chrysanthemums and coloured air-brushed spheres of modernism (*not* my design). The really fun part was just about to start. I had to figure out the logistics of transporting a 25-kilogram chocolate statue 300 miles to my home on Mull.

I must have forgotten about that fiasco, because last November I signed up for another chocolate class. I think that I can always improve my skills, and in turn Ninth Wave and our diners' experiences. Ruth Hinks is a UK World Chocolate Master and runs a lovely shop and school in Peebles called Cocoa Black. I thought that as this woman actually taught in Scotland (only one ferry, three trains and two buses away) it was too good to pass up. I've been making chocolates in my own little way for quite some time now and thought I could handle the master-class.

It was very well done and Ruth packed a lot of information and techniques into two days. For once I was at the top of the class with not a disaster in sight, and boy, did it feel good. I learned about inverted sugar syrups, molecular crystal alignment, praline pastes, conching and carraque. It was a great experience and Ruth and I had a ball tasting choccies together.

It is wonderful to have that knowledge to draw on, but I have stuck to my simple, old-fashioned organic methods for my ganache fillings and garnishes for Ninth Wave's chocolates, as it suits what we do here. I still make our choccies for the local Christmas fairs, and they can also be found on sale in the restaurant foyer, on Iona and in the village shop.

A Fresh Look at Cocktails

Since we opened we have always had a unique cocktail and drinks menu that I created myself. Many of the cocktails were invented on the premises, and can be found only at Ninth Wave.

For Scots the art of distilling is an integral part of their identity and cultural heritage. Whisky is the spirit we first think of in connection with Scotland, but in recent years many high quality small-batch gins have emerged in this country. Talented in utilising the flavourful ingredients so generously provided for them in their native landscape, Scots seem to be naturals at gin-making. In the effort to keep our cocktail menu fresh I have concocted a wee small-batch gin menu which showcases three different gins for our diners.

Croft Bramble Cocktail: The Botanist Gin, fresh lemon juice, agave syrup, Crème de mure, fresh bramble puree.

Gin Wave: a fresh breeze – Hendrick's Gin, cucumber, garden Mint, fresh lime and tonic.

Highland Fling: a vibrant cocktail using Caorunn Scottish gin, which is infused with a myriad of Celtic plants. Tonic, a splash of elderflower cordial, soda, a slice of apple and a sprig of bog myrtle enhance this small-batch gin.

Wild Raspberry Cocktail: a heady mix of The Botanist Gin, in-house pickled raspberries in syrup, tonic and fresh thyme.

GIN-PICKLED WILD RASPBERRIES

We love using the wild raspberries from our croft for this recipe, but brambles or blueberries are just as delicious. These lovely pickled gems feature in our Wild Raspberry Cocktail.

600ml/1 pt raspberries (added last)
wild thyme
bog myrtle
2 tbsp salt
3 Sichuan peppercorns
5 black peppercorns
3 juniper berries
¼ tsp dried galangal
5 tbsp sugar
300ml/10fl oz Scottish gin (The Botanist for preference)
100ml/3fl oz water

Pummel the dry ingredients in a mortar with a pestle to release the flavours.

Heat in a medium-sized pan over medium heat with the rest of the ingredients except for the gin. Just bring to the boil, mixing well to dissolve the sugar. Remove from the heat and let cool. Strain the cooled brine and add the gin. Divide the berries into sterilized jam jars and fill with the brine until the berries are completely covered. Cap the jars and refrigerate for two weeks before using.

Gin is made by mashing and steeping botanicals in a tasteless base spirit and distilling this in a pot still or a Carter-Head still, which each yield their own distinct product. With a tantalising list of native botanicals, the new breed of Scottish gin-makers have made Celtic versions of the original gin which was first produced in seventeenth-century Holland as a stomach medicine.

Exotics like orris root, calamus, cinnamon and coriander are still used, but are a mere backdrop for the likes of rowan berry, heather, bog myrtle, apple mint, gorse blossom and thyme; tastes foraged from the wild hills, peat bogs and seashores of Scotland.

As we rely heavily on fresh botanicals from our croft for flavour profiles, we like using these new botanical gins to enhance some of our menu dishes and to add another dimension to our unique cocktail menu. We use them to flavour sorbet, beef bordelaise sauce, pickles and infused berries.

Hendrick's Gin is a thoroughly Steampunk experience. This is a quirky and strange concoction which Hendrick's claims is 'made with a free and imaginative spirit.' This is a handcrafted gin rich in botanicals, including yarrow, chamomile and elderflower, but is dominated by the passion of Damascus roses and the green charm of cucumber. Its surprising taste is distilled in small batches of just 450 litres at a time by master distiller Lesley Gracie. Hendrick's is a combination of two different spirits which she creates in two rare and unusual stills: the Bennet still and the Carter-Head still, which in itself, sets it apart from other gins. A scintillating combination of exotics and native Scottish plants ensures this smooth gin can be sipped on its own, or works equally well in curious cocktails. Pour yourself some Hendrick's and browse their unusual website; you'll feel like you've embarked on a far-flung journey.

The Botanist is made on the Hebridean Isle of Islay, by Bruichladdich Distillery, noted for its long history of whisky-making. Nine traditional gin aromatics, including cassia bark and lemon peel, make a foundation for this artisan spirit. Appreciated for its spicy and floral bouquet, twenty-two local Islay botanicals, hand-foraged by an expert team, are crucial to the mix which makes it. Distilled at low-pressure, Islay's botanicals are slowly and softly coaxed into releasing their personalities. This seasonal mix is created in a still they call 'Ugly Betty' in an excruciatingly slow seventeen-hour distillation. This long drawn out infusion makes for a unique, citrus and floral gin with a long spicy finish. It is marketed as 'A breath of botanical Islay in every glass'.

Caorunn is a quality product handcrafted at the Balmenach distillery in Speyside. The smoothness of this gin is without the sharp edge and medicinal tinge of most gins. It is uniquely made from eleven botanicals and mineral-rich water from the Highland mountains. There are notes of apple and dandelion as well as a distinct hit of rowan berry that pops up from time to time. It has grassy undertones with a crisp wash of citrus. Unlike most gins, Caorunn uses pure grain spirit rather than molasses. It is distilled in small batches using a copper berry chamber to blend the tastes all of the essential botanicals together.

The Taste

One afternoon last August I was checking emails in the office (actually our living room, which is off from the kitchen) when something unusual caught my eye. The subject line 'AUDITIONS FOR CHANNEL 4 TV's "THE TASTE" ARE TAKING PLACE NOW! Somehow the producer had heard about us in our tiny corner of Mull and wanted me to apply to audition in Glasgow in September. 'Are you Britain's most naturally gifted cook? Contestants must please the palates of the judges Nigella Lawson, Anthony Bourdain and Ludo Lefebvre with just one spoonful of food. Tastings will be performed blind. It's all about Taste!'

No chance. Is this a joke? I'd never be able to get to Glasgow during the busy season. File it in the spam folder.

I walked back into the kitchen and told Fédra about the email. Her lovely face lit up, her green eyes sparkled and she exclaimed in her luscious Hungarian accent, 'Ooh! Thees eez wery exciting. You vill be on televeezon!'

'Well, no . . . there's no way with a fully-booked restaurant. I couldn't get away. I couldn't possibly.' Round-eyed, mouth open, 'Reeely? No?' Fédra asked, clearly downcast.

'No. Out of the question. Not going to happen. Would have been an adventure, though, wouldn't it?' I said, as I turned back to Fédra who had been rinsing garden greens at the sink. No Fédra.

Turning towards the door of the dining room I saw her with the bookings diary in hand, quickly flipping the pages. 'Eet eez great fortune. No persons booked for thees days!'

Sure enough, by a freak occurrence there was an empty window of three days which made it possible to create the food, get off the island to Glasgow, audition and then make it back before the next bookings.

After a day of Fédra's enthusiastic pleas not to miss this TV opportunity, I filled in the application form. I sent a Halloween photo of me in my pink Marie Antoinette wig. I wrote about my first food memory of stealing a piece of lemon meringue pie off the counter one morning as a baby, volunteered that my hobbies are virtual sumo wrestling and Steampunk and that I once wrote a poem dedicated to Nigella Lawson. There was no way I'd be hearing back from them.

The same day I got an email saying I'd passed the first hurdle, and could they phone me tomorrow?

Next day I got the phone call. A very nice guy chatted to me about Ninth Wave and our food and then announced, 'And now for the quiz!'

'*Quiz*?!' I burbled. Like a robot on overdrive he started rattling off questions. 'What are the ingredients of baba ganoush? What is salsify? What are ramsons? What city is bouillabaisse from? Describe osso buco?'

I am somewhat of a quiz addict and extremely competitive (Trivial Pursuit can become a full-contact sport in our house). The inquisition lasted about five minutes, but felt like ages. My one remaining brain cell was fizzling out and I wanted a cuppa badly, so I was ecstatic to hear the quiz master say that I'd done the best out of all the hundreds of those interviewed so far, getting every question right but one. I was going to audition in Glasgow after all.

I had to bring two dishes (to be served cold) which were cooked beforehand, and then plate them at the Station Hotel in front of the production team and cameras. No seafood was allowed, which cut out my favourite dishes from the restaurant. The logistics of travelling all the way from Fionnphort, across the ferry to Oban and three hours to Glasgow with food would be tricky.

Of course, I chose wisely. One dish would be my signature wild Fionnphort Venison Carpaccio. The other, a trio of meadowsweet desserts including, yes, *ice cream*. Why, why, why? Perhaps I thought no one else would dare.

During an interlude of serendipity at our local charity shop, I found a two miniature fridges that could be plugged into the cigarette lighter of a car. I hoped if I wrapped the ice cream in foil on top of a frozen gel-pack and didn't open the fridge door, it might last until my audition at 3 pm.

The car only had one cigarette lighter, so I had to play fridge roulette. Between Jonny the curmudgeon, muttering at highway signs (he hates motorways and we often end up in Stirling no matter where we are trying to get to) and me playing plug-in tag while trying to coax on a pair of fancy nylons over my more than ample body, it was one crazy ride.

We finally made it to Glasgow with hours to spare, and found our way to the correct co-ordinates (a conference room where half a dozen people were tiddling-up their plates of food on trestle tables). I wanted to make an impression. I was dressed in a rockabilly pencil dress with a 50s victory curl hairdo for the occasion. They were dressed in jeans. Holding my stomach in, I wobbled on my high heels to register at the check-in desk. I then plugged in my fridges, re-applied my Crimson Passion lipstick and waited. Everyone else in the room seemed so ordinary, except for a huge army guy who cooked with Irn Bru.

Finally I was called to start plating. Upon opening my mini fridges I was shocked. The ice cream was still frozen, the crisp garden greens had survived and the marinated venison was mouth-watering. I did not trip while going into the filming room with my dishes in hand. I answered questions as well as I could while watching them eat the meadowsweet panna cotta with chocolate sauce.

They asked if I was competitive. I said, 'My motto has always been, "It's not how you play the game, but whether you win or lose".' They asked if I had drive. I answered 'My husband Jonny and I created a high-end restaurant from a stone ruin at the end of the known universe, in a village of 120 people, from only imagination, supreme effort and blind faith, with not a penny in our pockets to start with. I think I have drive.'

I strove to be charming and enthusiastic, hoping that my quirkiness and passion would shine through. I thought I did my best. Perhaps I sounded manic? Maybe they detested my Canadian accent, which was once described as 'boggin' by a Scot? Was I too fat for television? Too opinionated?

'We'll let you know,' droned the faceless woman behind the camera.

And they did. I got a rejection email after a month-long wait. I was completely devastated. I cried into

ME — DRESSED UP.

my porridge and was inconsolable for days. I had lost the opportunity to put Ninth Wave on the map.

Like a continuous loop, I went over and over the film interview in my mind. What could I have done better, different? I should have lost weight. Was the cleavage too risqué? Did they not enjoy my anecdote of Jonny frolicking with his tubers in the garden? Did I try too hard?

The whole village was stunned, and Jane B., our emergency waitress, wasn't the only one to state in disbelief, 'I can't imagine anyone better suited to be on television! What were they thinking? What could they have possibly been looking for?' Jonny kindly said he thought I was too good, too professional for the competition.

But I have a feeling that perhaps, in the end, I was simply *too much*.

ON THE HEBRIDEAN HORIZON

Our hard work seems to be finally getting noticed by the powers that be who give out awards. Running a restaurant on the edge of the known universe might be picturesque, but is not conducive to getting press, reviews or awards of any kind.

Last year, for the first time, we applied for the Highland Food and Drink Awards and were pleased to make the shortlist for Restaurant of the Year 2013. We were also nominated as a finalist for the Environment Award. We were so chuffed to have made the finals; we were soon on our way in our beat-up Hilux fishing truck to the awards ceremony in Inverness. This was a welcome adventure after a busy season.

We pulled up to the Drummossie House Hotel and went inside to enjoy the evening. We found ourselves greeted at the door and ushered into a grand entrance room full of hundreds of people in their dazzling finery. Sequinned evening dresses vied with kilts and Bonnie Prince Charlie jackets, tuxes and tails with red satin gowns. There were so many people they spilled through a distant set of double doors into a vast mahogany-panelled room. Trays were brimming with champagne and colourful whisky cocktails.

Used to our village of a hundred or so people, this mammoth gathering left Jonny and I feeling a bit overwhelmed at first. But here we were, bubbly in hand and feeling hopeful. There was really nothing else for it, we were here to mingle amongst the glitterati of the Highland food and drink industries. 'Come on, we have to meet some people. We can't just stand here.' I said, dragging a dapper Jonny along with me.

Some groups seemed in the midst of heated debate, others had closed circles which would be awkward to lunge into. We were well into the far room before settling on a group of three decent-looking people who seemed unintimidating. We went for it, stepped forward and introduced ourselves. We were now in the company of a modest university lecturer, his wife and their friend Rita. The professor was presenting one of the awards that evening. We had a good chat about sourcing local produce in rural Scotland and other general topics. Our group photo had been taken by the hired press covering the event. Soon we were off to mingle a bit more before sitting down in the awards room. Jonny remarked, 'I've a feeling I know Rita's face.'

During the meal we sat with an odd assortment of great people, including an artisan beer store owner and a Liberace-type meat salesman named Vern. We were so excited, but had a healthy attitude of 'Don't expect to win; we're only here for a well-deserved knees-up.' We were up against some pretty heavy hitters. First and foremost, the Michelin-starred restaurant Boath House in Nairn and the well-known Whitehouse in Lochaline. We had the added bonus of competing in the most contested category of the awards. Butterflies was not the term to describe what I was feeling. It was more like a clog-dancing marmoset had invaded my stomach. I couldn't even finish my chocolate pudding, and that says it all.

Before we knew it, the awards ceremony began with much fanfare and lots of lights. With good grace we lost out in the environment category to a fellow Mull business, Island Bakery.

Sooner than expected our favourite category was announced and there we were on the massive stage screen, as a finalist for Restaurant of the Year. I felt quite nauseous. We'd been here before, having lost in the finals at the Scottish Thistle Awards the only time we entered them. And then I heard it, Fred Macaulay's voice booming, 'And the winner is . . . Ninth Wave Restaurant, Isle of Mull!'

I was no longer in control of my limbs. I shot skyward from the dining chair and screamed as if I was the next chosen contestant on 'The Price Is Right'

game show. I hugged Jonny so tight I almost throttled him. Disengaging my pink claws from his lapels, he said, 'Come now, we've got to get the award, lass.' And get it we did. Stunned and grinning like a demented version of the Mona Lisa I went up with Jonny, grabbed hold of that trophy and held on for dear life. Cameras whizzed and flashes flashed.

After the awards finished Rita came up to congratulate us. She pointedly looked into Jonny's face and said, 'You don't remember me do you?' Jonny replied that her face seemed familiar but he had no idea why. Then Rita went to explain that she'd been our secret dining judge for the awards. She'd been quite flabbergasted that we had charged straight through a room of 300 people to introduce ourselves to her. As I was in the kitchen on that particular night, I'd not met her previously. She went on to say how happy she was that we had won since we were her favourite. The description with which Fred had introduced our nomination was in fact Rita's words:

'It's not the easiest place in the world to get to, but the bumpy drive up the dirt track is well worth the effort when you discover the gem that is Ninth Wave waiting for you at the end like a mystical treasure trove. Inside, this small restaurant is contemporary but cosy with a kilted John Lamont doing the meeting, greeting and waiting. You probably won't see wife, Carla, however – she's hard at work in the kitchen, creating amazing menus that change daily depending on what fisherman John's caught that day! Combined with the freshest, seasonal produce grown outside on the couple's croft, the food is beautifully presented – an absolute treat for the taste-buds.'

Later that night when asked by one of the awards officials if we'd like a box to put our award in I answered, 'No thanks. I intend to wear it all evening.'

2013 was a phenomenal year. We also won the Regional Finals for the Scottish Thistle Awards Best Restaurant Category against all of Glasgow and Central South West Scotland. These awards are designed to discover and celebrate excellence and innovation by the Scottish tourism industry. We went to the gala evening at Stirling Castle and had a wonderful time. We've also been lucky enough to have marvellous customers who have made it possible to obtain Trip Advisor's 5-Star Excellence rating four years in a row.

At Ninth Wave we hope to help put Mull on the culinary map. We also plan to establish a Hebridean food trail for the Inner Isles and forge strong links with others excelling in this area's food industry. The main focus of all our endeavours will continue to be Ninth Wave with its croft and garden on this wild promontory of the Isle of Mull. The food, the service and the people are what's important. Of course press, marketing and awards are key to success, but we try to think of the essentials, the fine detail, the human elements. This, I hope, will keep our wonderful customers coming back to visit us.

We get busier every year, and are attracting destination diners despite our remote location. People are now finding out about Ninth Wave online and are booking months in advance, visiting Mull just to dine with us. What a compliment.

A good majority of Mull visitors stay in the north of the island in or near the capital of Tobermory. The Ross is Mull's unsung hero, with just a handful of visitors venturing down to stay in Fionnphort for a quieter stay. From Fionnphort there are local walks around Loch Pottie, to Knockvologan, Tor Mor Quarry and the ruined township of Braighcreich near Kintra. We do obtain some of our business with the help of the local B&B's and from passing trade. Many people dine at Ninth Wave on their way back from the glorious isles of Iona and Staffa. Happily, there are also increasing numbers of locals and visitors alike who are willing to make the four-hour round trip from Tobermory to eat here. Supporting local business is important to us, and we're glad we can start giving business back to the B&B's that have given us much custom, by guiding destination diners to their doors.

A few more things have changed since we first opened the doors at Ninth Wave. Jonny no longer runs into the dining room with only minutes to go, still madly fastening his sporran. He has honed his bartending prowess and waiting skills to something like professional standards, and now has the nous to keep out of the kitchen when my hair is standing on end.

From a city girl I have blossomed into a keen herb and flower gardener and avid forager. I have adopted an air of semi-maturity, having come a long way from sitting in a heap on the kitchen floor, a spatula in one hand and a roll of paper towel in the other wailing, 'I can't do it. I just can't do it!'

The garden grows bigger and the croft wilder. We take pleasure in greeting more return customers with each season. Jonny grows older, but none the wiser.

We have swapped the tin bath for a Victorian roll-top, a peat fire for posh under-floor heating and are, in many ways, far removed from that rusty-roofed shed where Jonny and I ate our first meal together. I remember the taste of that magic mouthful of buttered lobster, and most certainly am still in love with, first, the rugged fisherman, the island and its food.

BIOGRAPHIES

 **Carla Lamont** (nee Jetko) is a writer, poet and self-taught chef, born in Regina, Saskatchewan, Canada. Her family moved to the island city of Victoria, British Columbia, when she was twelve. She started her cooking career as a weekend pizza chef at the age of fourteen. Carla came to the UK to work on the Isle of Iona at the bohemian circus that was the Argyll Hotel. She met her husband Jonny soon after and came to live at the croft near Fionnphort. They got married on the fishing pier at Carsaig, Mull, to the skirl of the bagpipes, in 1996. An award-winning poet, her collection *The Body Banquet* was published in 2006.

 **Dr Samantha ('Sam') Jones** is a professional landscape photographer whose home has been on the Isle of Mull since 1998. Educated in Law at the London School of Economics (LSE) and the University of Oxford, Sam previously worked in government in London, Belfast and Edinburgh. She now spends her time capturing the magical play of Hebridean light on land, sea and loch. Through her photography she seeks to convey a sense of place and a sense of being there, of experiencing the elements and the landscape. Sam was RNLI Photographer of the Year in 2011, commended in the Landscape Photographer of the Year competition in 2012 and a finalist in the Scottish Nature Photography Awards in 2013. Sam also has a huge appetite, particularly for Asian and Middle Eastern food, and so working on the Ninth Wave Restaurant book has been the ultimate photographic pleasure. (Photo of Sam by Alastair James Macleod.)

 THANKS

Every success Ninth Wave has enjoyed is because of our stalwart team of lovely staff.

Thanks to all our friends/employees past and present. Special thanks to:

Steve Illes, tractor repairman, handyman and hydraulic engineer.
Kirsty Lamont, sous-chef, public relations, artist, daughter.
Fiona McLean, aesthetic and antiseptic engineer.
Amanda Noddings, waitress extraordinaire.
(Alexandra) Fédra Plavecz, sous-chef, tea-maker and general good egg.
Dr Janet Schofield, the 'dishwasher with a doctorate'.
Jane the Diver, painter and emergency waitress.
Jane Brunton, emergency waitress and moral support.
Catriona Mackie, waitress and lovely local lass.

Also special mention to all my brothers (for monetary and recipe support) and my sister Jan who bravely came to help us open the restaurant and worked 16-hour shifts for weeks with only sticky toffee pudding as payment.

We are grateful for all the support and custom we have received from many of our local B&B's and other businesses on Mull and Iona. Thanks to Sarah Blackwell for so kindly proof-reading and editing the text and recipes for me.

OPPOSITE, CLOCKWISE FROM TOP LEFT: CATRIONA, KIRSTY AND CARLA, JANE B, AMANDA, JANET, FÉDRA, STEVE, JANE THE DIVER, FIONA.

LOCAL SUPPLIERS

We are very lucky to have a wide variety of great quality food suppliers on Mull. Here are contact details for a few of them which you may find useful.

Ardalanish Beef, Ardalanish: 01681 700674
Admore Fish, Salen: 01681 300468
Dail an Inbhire Organic Farm and Shop, Kintra: 01681 700509
Inverlussa Mussels, Craignure: 01680 812436
Isle of Mull Crab Company, Dervaig: 01688 400364
Isle of Mull Oysters, Dervaig: 01688 400268
Knockvologan Lamb, Fionnphort: 01681 700372
Scriob Ruadh Farm Cheeses and Pork, Tobermory: 01688 302235
Tobermory Fish, Tobermory: 01688 302120
Treshnish Farm Beef and Lamb, Treshnish: 01688 400425

RECIPE INDEX

JONNY'S BOAT (KIRSTY LAMONT)